14148

CAN WE BE NEUTRAL?

PUBLICATIONS OF THE
COUNCIL ON FOREIGN RELATIONS

FOREIGN AFFAIRS (*quarterly*), edited by Hamilton Fish Armstrong.

SURVEY OF AMERICAN FOREIGN RELATIONS (*in four volumes,* 1928-1931), prepared under the direction of Charles P. Howland.

THE UNITED STATES IN WORLD AFFAIRS (*annual*). Volumes for 1931, 1932 and 1933 by Walter Lippmann and William O. Scroggs. Volume for 1934-1935 by Whitney H. Shepardson and William O. Scroggs.

POLITICAL HANDBOOK OF THE WORLD (*annual*), edited by Walter H. Mallory.

INTERNATIONAL SECURITY, The American Rôle in Collective Action for Peace. By Philip C. Jessup.

THE FOREIGN POLICY OF THE POWERS, by Jules Cambon, Richard von Kühlmann, Sir Austen Chamberlain, Dino Grandi, Viscount Ishii, Karl Radek and John W. Davis.

ORES AND INDUSTRY IN SOUTH AMERICA, by H. Foster Bain and Thomas Thornton Read.

ORES AND INDUSTRY IN THE FAR EAST, by H. Foster Bain.

FOREIGN AFFAIRS BIBLIOGRAPHY, 1919-1932. By William L. Langer and Hamilton Fish Armstrong.

THE RECOVERY OF GERMANY, by James W. Angell.

EUROPE: THE WORLD'S BANKER, 1870-1914, by Herbert Feis.

DIRECTORY OF AMERICAN AGENCIES CONCERNED WITH THE STUDY OF INTERNATIONAL AFFAIRS, compiled by Ruth Savord.

CAN WE BE NEUTRAL?

BY
ALLEN W. DULLES
AND
HAMILTON FISH ARMSTRONG

PUBLISHED BY HARPER & BROTHERS, NEW YORK, FOR
COUNCIL ON FOREIGN RELATIONS, INC.
45 EAST 65TH STREET · NEW YORK

COUNCIL ON FOREIGN RELATIONS

OFFICERS AND DIRECTORS

ELIHU ROOT
Honorary President

NORMAN H. DAVIS
Vice-President

WHITNEY H. SHEPARDSON
Treasurer

GEORGE W. WICKERSHAM
President

EDWIN F. GAY
Vice-President

ALLEN W. DULLES
Secretary

WALTER H. MALLORY
Executive Director

FRANK ALTSCHUL
HAMILTON FISH ARMSTRONG
ISAIAH BOWMAN
PAUL D. CRAVATH
JOHN W. DAVIS
HAROLD W. DODDS

STEPHEN P. DUGGAN
PHILIP C. JESSUP
RUSSELL C. LEFFINGWELL
WALTER LIPPMANN
GEORGE O. MAY
FRANK L. POLK

OWEN D. YOUNG

COMMITTEE ON RESEARCH

ISAIAH BOWMAN
Chairman

HAMILTON FISH ARMSTRONG
H. FOSTER BAIN
ALLEN W. DULLES

EDWIN F. GAY
WALTER LIPPMANN
WHITNEY H. SHEPARDSON

2nd Edition (2nd printing)
Copyright, 1936, by Council on Foreign Relations, Inc.
Printed in the United States of America

PREFACE TO SECOND EDITION

Early in 1934 the Council on Foreign Relations began considering whether it was practicable, by modifying the accepted neutrality policy of the United States, to avoid some of the disputes which in the past have involved the country in war.

This volume attempts to give the pros and cons of the various courses open to the country, viewing these in the light of past experience, in their relation to the larger problem of world peace, and above all with reference to their practicability and expediency.

The authors have gained much from the discussions held at the Council House. But the views they express are their own, and are not to be attributed to other members of the Council individually or to the Council itself. The Council's only responsibility lies in having decided that such a volume as this might usefully be written and published at a moment when the subject of neutrality was attracting wide attention.

The authors are grateful to the members of the Research Committee for valuable comment. They also are much indebted to the staff of the Council—especially to Mr. William O. Scroggs, Director of Research, for material on the American experience during the Napoleonic Wars and for the trade statistics included in the Appendix, and to Miss Ruth Savord, Librarian, for the Bibliography. Miss Mary H. Stevens and Miss Olga Schierloh have helped with the proofs and in many other ways.

This second edition is a duplicate of the first (published January 1936) except that it includes in an Addendum the text of the Joint Resolution extending and amending the Neutrality Act of August 31, 1935, passed by the House on February 17, 1936, by the Senate on February 18, and signed by the President on February 29. Section 1 is effective only until May 1, 1937, so that further legislation presumably will be considered before that date.

A. W. D.
H. F. A.

New York, February 29, 1936

"The occasion is not of our own making. We had no part in making it. But it is here. It affects us as directly and palpably almost as if we were participants in the circumstances which gave rise to it.... We shall pay the bill, though we did not deliberately incur it."

—WOODROW WILSON, Address to Congress, September 4, 1914.

CONTENTS

I. NEUTRALITY: POLICY NOT LAW   1
II. EARLY TESTS OF OUR NEUTRALITY POLICY
    1. Neutral Rights and Neutral Duties   11
    2. Failure to Keep Out of War in 1812   14
III. NEUTRALITY FAILS IN 1917   20
IV. THE NEUTRALITY ACT OF 1935   35
V. WHY CONGRESS ACTED   44
VI. PRESIDENT ROOSEVELT'S INTERPRETATION OF THE ACT   58
VII. OUR FUTURE NEUTRALITY POLICY
    1. Basic Neutrality   77
    2. Travel in War Zones   79
    3. The Arms Embargo   81
    4. Loans and Credits   85
VIII. TRADE AND PEACE
    1. A Mandatory Embargo on Trade   91
    2. "Trade at Your Own Risk"   104
    3. Moral Suasion   107
    4. Quotas   110
    5. "Cash and Carry"   112
IX. CONCLUSION
    1. Avoiding War   114
    2. Maintaining Peace   117

Appendices

1. President Wilson's Proclamation of Neutrality, August 4, 1914 — 123
2. President Wilson's Statement of August 19, 1914 — 130
3. The Act of April 13, 1934 (the "Johnson Act") — 132
4. United States Neutrality Laws, as Revised to January 3, 1935 — 133
5. The Neutrality Act of August 31, 1935 — 143
6. President Roosevelt's Statement of August 31, 1935 — 150
7. Secretary Hull's Statement of September 12, 1935 — 152
8. President Roosevelt's Proclamation of October 5, 1935, Concerning the Export of Arms, Ammunition, and Implements of War to Ethiopia and Italy — 156
9. President Roosevelt's Proclamation of October 5, 1935, Concerning Travel by American Citizens on Vessels of Belligerent Nations — 160
10. A Note on Previous American Embargoes of Arms Shipments — 162
11. Key War Materials: Percentages of World Production, 1929, by Countries — 165
12. Changes in American Export Trade, 1913-1934 — 166
13. American Exports of Certain War Materials to Italy, 1934-1935 — 167

Addenda

1. Draft Neutrality Bill, Introduced January 3, 1936, by Senator Pittman and Mr. McReynolds — 168
2. Joint Resolution Extending and Amending the Neutrality Act of August 31, 1935, signed by President Roosevelt February 29, 1936 — 179

Bibliography on American Neutrality — 181

Index — 188

CHAPTER I

NEUTRALITY:
POLICY NOT LAW

THE American people have an overwhelming desire to remain at peace with the rest of the world. They say that it is worth almost any sacrifice to keep free of other peoples' wars. But did they not have very much the same feeling in the days preceding the War of 1812 and in the opening phases of the World War? On neither occasion, as it turned out, were they willing to pay the price of peace, either in loss of trade or diminished national prestige. The wars in Europe became our wars.

Will it be different tomorrow if the country finds itself faced with similar problems and a similar choice? Those who hope that it will be different must consider how high a price the American people are really prepared to pay, in practice, for some measure of added protection. They should not let the idea gain currency that the price can be paid painlessly, or underestimate the difficulty of persuading the American people to pay it, or imagine that absolute security can be bought even if the country determines to make every legitimate sacrifice. That way lie false hopes, false optimism, and in the end disaster.

Many books have been written on neutrality in its historical and legal aspects. We do not propose to deal with the subject from either point of view. The historical neutrality which nations have attempted to maintain almost from the days of chivalry has little practical significance in a world where wars are fought as they are fought today. The legalistic conception of neutrality, and particularly of neutral rights, is based on precedents which had long been confused and weakened by the successively different and inconsistent positions which nations had taken, depending upon whether they expected to be or happened to be neutrals or belligerents. During the World War an American asked an eminent English authority why, when the Declaration of London was being elaborated in 1909, England, reversing her traditional position, favored curtailing the right of a belligerent to interfere with neutral shipping. The answer was: "We expected to be neutral in the next war." And how often we ourselves found in 1914-1917, when we wanted to make good some argument against British trade restrictions, that Great Britain was only taking a leaf out of the book of our own Civil War policies. Final blows to many of the legal formulae of neutrality were delivered in the World War, and those that remained were further complicated by the changes in the relationship of belligerent and neutral produced by the Covenant of the League of Nations and by the Briand-Kellogg Pact.[1]

Almost any policy of neutrality will serve in a minor conflict. But the policy which the American Government adopts when the great sea powers of the world are combatants is of overwhelming importance—for by it may ultimately be decided the question of peace or war, involving the comfort, happiness and perhaps the lives of innumerable American citizens. Our purpose, then, is to make a realistic and non-technical examination of the present position of the United States, in the hope of contributing to the study of the alternative courses of action open to our Government in case the nations of the world with which it has close relations go to war. Decisions are about to be taken that no shouted injunctions over the radio ought to influence, that deserve better than part-time consideration by an unwieldy Congressional committee and partisan

---

[1] The Covenant modified the old conception of neutrality as between signatory states and a member of the League judged an aggressor. The view that the Briand-Kellogg Pact had altered the relations of nations was expressed by Secretary of State Stimson, speaking before the Council on Foreign Relations, New York, August 8, 1932. As a result of the Pact, he said, war becomes "an illegal thing. Hereafter when two nations engage in armed conflict either one or both of them must be wrongdoers—violators of the general treaty. We no longer draw a circle about them and treat them with the punctilios of the duelist's code. Instead, we denounce them as lawbreakers. By that very act we have made obsolete many legal precedents and have given the legal profession the task of reëxamining many of its codes and treaties." (*Foreign Affairs*, v. 11, no. 1, Supplement.)

debate in the final hectic sessions of a dying Congress.

We are often reminded that in 1914 we were unprepared for war. By this is generally meant that we were not ready in a military way to uphold our rights promptly in the face of any serious challenge. This is true, at least with regard to the enforcement of our will overseas. But looking back we see now that our lack of preparedness was not military only. We were not prepared as a neutral with any policy which held out a reasonable hope that in a protracted conflict between great protagonists we could remain safely aside. Popular opinion and to some extent official opinion were deluded with the idea that there was a well-defined and accepted status known as "neutrality," and that if we obeyed certain rules known to the initiate, even if not to the man in the street, we could keep out of war. We further expected that, with certain minor restrictions, we could continue to enjoy normal liberties of travel and trade. We had no way of foretelling the scope and application of the new methods and instruments of warfare in ruthless hands. We could not foresee the "war zones" on the high seas, the sowing of mines on the open seas, the unrestricted submarine warfare, or other unprecedented actions which largely did away with the geographical limitations on war. Nor did we foresee the criminal acts of violence on our own territory. Despite our known deficiencies in military equipment we felt in 1914 that in almost any contingencies our economic strength would force even from belligerents a respect for what we conceived to be our rights.

The experience of the period 1914-1917 should have brought us to an earlier awakening. We should have begun long before this a careful examination of the problems facing us as a would-be neutral. Unfortunately during the decade and a half following "the war that was to end wars" the country was under the spell of the philosophy that the world had learnt its lesson and that serious threats to world peace had been eliminated, at least for the lifetime of those who had survived. We were busy recouping our losses and planning new commercial and scientific triumphs. In many circles it was considered almost improper to speak of war as a possibility. As far as our relations with the rest of the world were concerned, many felt that the only task was to consolidate more fully the peace which had been won, and that sufficient means to this end could be found in the limitation and control of armaments, Briand-Kellogg Pacts, *ad hoc* collaboration with other nations on specific issues, and the friendly if not very precise attitude called the policy of "the good neighbor."

What happened in Manchuria was a shock and a warning. The Ethiopian crisis again brought us up short. We have seen two of the seven major powers of the world actually engaged in conducting hostilities. We have had warning from the leader of one of the others that he is merely biding the propitious moment to take what he thinks his country needs, peacefully if nobody opposes, if necessary by force.

These and other developments bring home to us the need for a clearer conception of our position. The Ethiopian crisis provided the incentive for us to think out a new policy of neutrality. We may some day look back with gratitude to the fact that the opportunity for debate and experiment came in a situation which had not yet assumed the proportions of a world disaster. But we must be careful not to assume that future wars will resemble the Italo-Ethiopian war, or imagine that if we legislate with that particular situation in view we shall have provided a satisfactory basis for dealing with other conflicts involving entirely different problems and presenting different dangers.

It is a mistake to brush aside the neutrality problem in an easy belief that the aversion to war now widely expressed in this country represents a fixed and permanent attitude. There also was aversion to war on the eve of our momentous decisions of 1812 and 1917. The feeling today is obviously sincere. From surface indications it promises to be lasting. But to believe this is to believe that the present generation of Americans differs fundamentally from preceding generations. War still has its glamor for those who have not seen it close and plain; and greatness, power and pride do not make a nation reasonable, careful and punctilious about the sensibilities and rights of others. That we feel strong does not mean that we have yet reached the degree of detachment and self-restraint suggested by the phrase "too proud to fight." We will not tolerate being flouted. In the future as in the past, we will presumably hold to what we believe to be our rights; and we will fight to maintain them if it is necessary. Not more than any other people are we immune to a war fever. For a country so isolated geographically we have indulged in more than our share of wars. Our press is free; but some of the most widely-read organs have been known to appeal to prejudice, low instincts and the mob spirit. The best we can hope to secure from any neutrality policy is to avoid as many as possible of the incidents that might arouse public feeling, and in the pursuit of this aim to avoid the assertion of rights which are not well-founded and fundamental, and which, once asserted, may involve our national honor and prestige.

The popular American conception that neutrality is a clearly defined status is erroneous. On the contrary, we shall come closer to a correct view if we think of neutrality merely as a policy which, within certain limits, has an almost infinite number of permutations and combinations. As a neutral, we can adopt a policy which indirectly but none the less substantially influences the course of hostilities between other nations by making the American reservoir of goods and raw materials available to those contestants who can receive them; or we can withdraw from commerce where the risk seems too great, as Jefferson tried to do in the early days of the nineteenth century. We can insist on certain so-called neutral rights as we did during the World War; or we can waive those rights, as many of the European neutrals were forced to do during the same period.

We are often told by eminent counsellors to adopt a sane neutrality or a strict neutrality or an impartial neutrality. All the terms are equally meaningless. No two authorities can agree on a definition of the precise rights and duties of neutrals, except as regards specific and for us minor matters such as the withholding of direct aid by a neutral government to a belligerent, or the duty of a neutral government to refuse to allow its territory to be used as a base for military operations against a belligerent. The trade rights of a neutral are as broad as the power the neutral is willing and able to assert to maintain those rights. If it is unable or unwilling to exert power, those rights are wholly at the mercy of the belligerent and exist only in so far as the belligerent does not find it expedient to curtail them. In fact, they are not rights at all in the sense that we speak of rights in domestic law, where there are courts and impartial agencies for enforcement.

The time has come to stop talking about the alleged virtues of neutrality and to turn our attention to the concrete question of planning the general policy which promises to be most expedient for the country to follow in the event war breaks out between other powers. We cannot foresee who will be at war and what they will be fighting for in any particular circumstance; but we can get some general principles clearly in mind and determine to stick to them as long as they serve our national interests. Only so will we be dealing with the realities of the modern world and escape from the futile task of furbishing up some old concept of a law of neutrality as dead as Caesar, with only a ghost to haunt us. In the following pages we shall continue to use the word "neutrality." But it is used in the sense of *that policy which a country at peace adopts toward countries at war.* It will not be used as connoting a status defined under international law.

We have come a long way in our thinking since 1914, and we seem now to be realizing that our neutrality policy should be shaped with a view to keeping us out of war rather than toward building up machinery to enable us to exact observance of so-called rights of trade. But we must be careful not to be misled by the ease of formulating abstract programs for the relinquishment of American rights. Such programs may sound satisfactory enough and may even find wide acceptance—until the shoe begins to pinch. But when the time comes actually to try to stop a certain class of exports, whether by moral suasion or by embargo, then we will realize that what is theoretically sound as a war-avoidance policy may be quite unacceptable to hard-pressed agricultural or industrial interests. If that happens, we shall have received one more demonstration that the United States is not yet an economically independent unit, that its prosperity is tied up with the markets of the world, and that voluntarily to step out of international trade may take more fortitude than is possessed by the political powers then in control of our national destinies.

Such, at least, is the lesson to be read in our history—once in the early days when our nation was young and a comparatively unimportant factor in the plans of Europe, once again when we had become a world power in the full sense of the term.

CHAPTER II

EARLY TESTS OF OUR NEUTRALITY POLICY

1. *Neutral Rights and Neutral Duties*

No country perhaps was ever so thoroughly against war as ours. These dispositions pervade every description of its citizens, whether in or out of office. They cannot perhaps suppress their affections nor their wishes. But they will suppress the effects of them so as to preserve a fair neutrality. Indeed, we shall be more useful as neutrals than as parties by the protection which our flag will give to supplies of provision.[1]

These were the words of Thomas Jefferson, Secretary of State in Washington's Cabinet, writing on April 20, 1793, to Gouverneur Morris, the American Minister to France. Only two months earlier war had broken out between Great Britain and France, the first in a series of conflicts following the French Revolution. With only brief intermissions they continued over a period of twenty-two years and gave the newly established American Government ample opportunity to formulate and test its own policy of neutrality.

Europe seemed so remote in those days of sailing vessels that at first there was little fear that the United States would be drawn into the conflict. Thus Jefferson's note reveals a twofold purpose: not only

[1] P. L. Ford, ed., "The Writings of Thomas Jefferson," v. VI, p. 217.

to keep out of the war, but to continue trading impartially with all the belligerents. Although he abhorred war, Jefferson was quite willing that the United States as a neutral should derive whatever benefits it could from the struggles abroad. "Since it is so decreed by fate," he wrote on hearing rumors of an impending war in Europe, "we have only to pray their soldiers may eat a great deal." In another letter he expressed the hope that "the new world will fatten on the follies of the old." [2]

But since this was a war between maritime powers, there was grave danger that the navies of the belligerents would inflict serious injury on the rapidly growing commerce of the United States. Not only was there danger of the violation of American neutral rights, but there was also danger that foreign agents of the belligerents and their sympathizers in the United States might compromise the country's neutrality through their efforts to assist one or the other of the warring powers. "Citizen" Genet, the new minister from the French Republic, had arrived in the United States soon after the outbreak of war in Europe and proceeded at once to commission privateers to war on British shipping.

This situation prompted President Washington, after a full discussion of the matter with his Cab-

---

[2] Quoted in Charles M. Thomas, "American Neutrality in 1793," p. 15-16.

inet, to issue his neutrality proclamation of April 22, 1793. This brief and simply worded document does not even mention the word "neutrality," but it is generally regarded by students of international law as a highly important step in the development of a new phase of the doctrine of neutrality. For instead of emphasizing neutral rights, the proclamation urged that citizens of the United States "should with sincerity and good faith adopt and pursue a conduct friendly and impartial toward the belligerent powers," and "avoid all acts and proceedings whatsoever, which may in any manner tend to contravene such disposition." Americans were warned that by aiding or abetting hostilities against any of the belligerents or "by carrying to any of them those articles which are deemed contraband by the *modern* usage of nations," they would forfeit their rights to the protection of the United States, and that those who violated the law of nations, "within the cognizance of the courts of the United States," would be prosecuted.[3]

The proclamation represented a distinct advance over the previous attitude of other governments toward the duties and obligations of neutrals. And its basic principles have since been generally accepted as the proper code of conduct for nonbelligerent nations in time of war. The next step of the American Government was the enactment of

[3] "American State Papers. Foreign Relations," v. I, p. 140.

a statute conferring authority on Federal officers to enforce the policy indicated in President Washington's proclamation. This was accomplished by the Neutrality Act of 1794, which forbade recruiting in the United States for foreign powers or the fitting out and arming of vessels for service against any belligerent state with which the United States was at peace. The essential features of this measure were embodied in the more inclusive Act of 1818, prescribing what are still the basic principles of the nation's duty as a neutral.

2. *Failure to Keep Out of War in* 1812

The American Government was soon compelled to shift its attention from neutral duties to neutral rights. The European war had not been in progress many months before the British Government, by its Orders in Council, began the seizure of American vessels on the high seas. Great Britain invoked the Rule of War of 1756, by which she had declared that trade which was forbidden to neutrals in time of peace should not be open to them in time of war, and she began seizing vessels trading between the United States and the French West Indies. By an order of November 6, 1793, the British Government directed the seizure of all ships carrying the produce of any French colony or carrying provisions or supplies to such a colony. This order led Congress in

March 1794 to impose the first of its embargoes on vessels in American ports planning to sail for foreign ports. This was a temporary embargo and was in effect for only sixty days; but instead of being conducive to peace it seemed to accelerate the drift toward war with Great Britain. A breach with that country was prevented by the Jay Treaty, which though very unpopular was at least a palliative.

The Jay Treaty, however, gave deep offense to France. By the Franco-American Treaty of 1778 France and the United States had already agreed that foodstuffs should not be regarded as contraband and that enemy goods should be safe under a neutral flag. The terms of the Jay Treaty, in the eyes of the French, conflicted with these provisions and were regarded by the French Government as a violation of American neutrality. The French Government thereupon adopted a retaliatory policy, which in 1798 brought the United States into actual, though undeclared, naval war with France. When Napoleon came into power in 1800 some of the differences between the United States and France were adjusted. In March 1802, the European war was stopped for the time being by the Peace of Amiens, and the neutrals obtained a breathing spell. Fourteen months later war broke out afresh and was conducted by both sides with even less regard than before for the rights of neutral nations.

In spite of the depredations on American commerce, the neutrality policy from 1793 to 1805 yielded handsome returns to American citizens; but as encroachments by both belligerents increased, it became more difficult to continue to walk the tight rope. It was impossible for a relatively small and weak nation like the United States of that day effectively to call both offenders to account. Furthermore, Thomas Jefferson, who was now President, was by sentiment a pacifist, and his pacifism took the form of deep resentment against the belligerents for the annoyance caused those who desired to remain at peace. In a letter to Livingston, our newly appointed Minister to France, Jefferson in 1801 set forth his philosophy:

War between two nations cannot diminish the rights of the rest of the world remaining at peace. The doctrine that the rights of nations remaining quietly in the exercise of moral and social duties are to give way to the convenience of those who prefer plundering and murdering one another, is a monstrous doctrine; and ought to yield to the more rational law, that "the wrong which two nations endeavor to inflict on each other, must not infringe on the rights or conveniences of those remaining at peace." And what is *contraband*, by the law of nature? Either everything which may aid or comfort an enemy, or nothing. Either all commerce which would accommodate him is unlawful, or none is. The difference between articles of one or another description, is a difference in degree only. No line between them can be drawn. Either all intercourse must cease between neutrals and belligerents, or all be permitted. Can the world hesitate to say which shall be the rule? Shall two nations turning tigers, break up in one instant the peaceable relations of the whole world? Reason and nature clearly pronounce that the neutral is to go on in the enjoyment of all its rights, that its commerce remains free, not subject to the jurisdiction of another, nor consequently its vessels to search, or to inquiries whether their contents are the property of an enemy, or are of those which have been called contraband of war.[4]

Unfortunately this is a picture of the world as it should be rather than of the world as it is. Jefferson's analysis of the unreality of the rule about contraband is almost prophetic; but his belief that the "rights" of the neutrals must prevail over the "necessity" of the belligerents was as unjustified in the early part of the nineteenth century as similar beliefs proved to be a hundred years later. Jefferson himself was soon to become the unfortunate victim of this discovery. Finding that the nations at war did infringe on the rights and conveniences of those remaining at peace, he still believed that commercial retaliation if applied impartially might compel the belligerent to listen to his protests and at the same time permit the country to remain basically neutral. The outcome was the Embargo Act of December 22, 1807, which has been called a "great experiment in pacifism." It failed to work as Jefferson had hoped and brought him only chagrin and disappointment.

[4] "The Works of Thomas Jefferson." Federal Edition, v. IX, p. 299.

The embargo did not bring Great Britain and France to accept the American idea of neutrality, but it cut our exports from $108,000,000 (the abnormal war-profiteering high) to $22,000,000.[5] It provoked Napoleon to retaliate by ordering the seizure of all American vessels found in ports under French jurisdiction, on the pretext that he was aiding the American Government in the suppression of unlawful commerce. It created such intense economic disturbance in New England—where it was openly violated—that secession was openly discussed. And it finally aroused such opposition throughout the whole country, and was so difficult to enforce, that a Congress controlled by Jefferson's own party repealed it in the last month of his term. The Embargo Act was replaced by the Non-Intercourse Act permitting trade with all countries except Great Britain and France. The President was authorized to resume commercial relations with whichever of these countries should first remove its restrictions against American trade. Napoleon took advantage of this stipulation. He revoked certain of his decrees; but this was a pretense, because he gave secret orders for the seizure of every American ship found in the ports under his control.

Thereupon, on May 1, 1810, Congress repealed the Non-Intercourse Act but stipulated that if either

---

[5] John Dickinson, "Neutrality and Commerce." *Proceedings of the American Society of International Law,* April 25-27, 1935, p. 112.

the British or the French Government should revoke its orders and decrees affecting American trade, the United States would prohibit commerce with the country still adhering to such restrictions. This measure further encouraged Napoleon to continue his efforts to convince the United States Government that he had in fact revoked his objectionable decrees and hence that it should suspend commercial relations with Great Britain.

As a result of the continued attacks on American commerce by Great Britain and France, a "war party" steadily gained strength in Congress. The United States had equally good reasons for declaring war against either of the belligerents. Napoleon's tortuous course was perhaps even worse than Britain's frank disregard of our neutral rights; but the offenses committed by Great Britain were the greater in quantity, due to her increasing control of the seas. In consequence, public resentment was greatest against the British. On June 1, 1812, President Madison sent a message to Congress declaring that Great Britain had abandoned "all respect for the neutral rights of the United States," and on June 18 Congress made a formal declaration of war. The policy of attempted insulation had been tried and found wanting.

CHAPTER III

NEUTRALITY FAILS IN 1917

IN THE opening decade of the twentieth century, unbeknownst to many Americans, the United States had become a world power. In 1908 it was still possible for a book by a distinguished historian to attract unusual attention merely because its title recognized the fact.[1]

The country's foreign trade had been growing by leaps and bounds; by 1913 exports reached a value of nearly two and a half billion dollars. Exports which bulked so large in the national economy exercised, of course, a correspondingly important political influence at Washington. Today we tend to forget this fact. In the last two decades the American export trade has been changing drastically in character, and its influence has changed with it. Our cotton exports have decreased roughly from 8,500,000 bales in 1913 to 6,000,000 bales in 1934, and our wheat and flour exports have decreased from 155,000,000 bushels in 1913 to 36,500,000 bushels in 1934. Since cotton and wheat are commodities which play a chief role in American politics, our foreign trade had far more political significance in 1914 than it has today, with cotton exports down

[1] "The United States as a World Power," by Archibald Cary Coolidge, was the first comprehensive survey of the country's new international position.

by more than a quarter and wheat exports dwindling to almost nothing. Today it is the industrialists who have the biggest stake in our trade with other nations; automobile makers, oil producers and others often exercise an important influence on domestic legislation; but their interest in general policies is not homogeneous and, due to the fact that a sparsely settled agricultural state has as many Senators as a populous industrial one, has not yet proved so effective politically as has the interest of the agrarian bloc.[2]

This digression has been introduced merely to indicate that in viewing the factors which led us to adopt a vigorous policy in defense of trade in the opening phases of the World War we must take account of the different conditions then existing. Of course we must not imagine that today our cotton growers or our farmers have abandoned hope of regaining some of their lost foreign markets or that they would not resist measures which deprived them of any part of the export trade that still remains. Nevertheless, a program which proposed restricting our foreign trade in wartime in order to avoid disputes regarding it might meet somewhat less political opposition now than twenty years ago.

[2] Though our exports of manufactured goods are less than they were in the boom days of 1929, they nevertheless are higher than they were twenty years ago. The changes in the composition of American foreign trade from 1913 to 1934 is shown in Appendix 12.

We have already suggested that we were unprepared as a people and as a government to deal with the conditions created by a general European war. There was no time in the summer of 1914 to sit down quietly to weigh the consequences of alternative courses to meet a situation which daily became more complicated, much less to think out a long-range policy. All that our Government could do was cling to the best precedents available, even though second thought might have raised doubts as to whether they really were applicable to the new conditions of maritime warfare, especially when the war was being waged by the mighty antagonists now locked in a death grip. We stuck to the precedents; and they led us step by step nearer the arena.

Several enlightening books on the period of our neutrality have recently appeared, among them the fifth volume of Woodrow Wilson's "Life and Letters," edited by Ray Stannard Baker; the "War Memoirs of Robert Lansing;" "American Diplomacy during the World War" and "American Neutrality: 1914-1917" by Charles Seymour; and Walter Millis's "Road to War: America, 1914-1917."

Mr. Millis's interesting book has exercised an important influence on current opinion. The impression it gives is that the United States was caught in the World War primarily because of the preponderance of British propaganda, the subtleties of British diplomacy, and the influence of vested financial, commercial and industrial interests whose fortunes became tied up with an Allied victory. These factors all counted. But to single them out and stress them so heavily seems to us to allow too little for the natural predisposition of many Americans for certain principles and their antipathy for certain others, for what Winston Churchill has called "the rhythm of tragedy"—the cumulative effect on the public conscience of that vast interplay of fact and sentiment from the day the German armies crossed the Belgian frontier in August 1914 with the watchword "necessity knows no law," until President Wilson, addressing the Senate on April 2, 1917, set a public seal on his reluctant decision: "The present German submarine warfare against commerce is a warfare against mankind. It is a war against all nations." Mr. Millis, it seems to us, tends to ignore the fundamental reasons why American sentiment turned in favor of the Allies and against Germany.[3] It is not necessary to hunt for a demon

[3] Thus one looks in vain for a reference to the fact that there was a treaty guaranteeing Belgium, that Germany had signed it, and that Germany's violation of it exercised an instantaneous and persistent effect on American feeling toward Germany. The Belgian deportations are called an "attack upon the unemployment problem in Belgium and Northern France;" it is not mentioned that in 1917 Germany ordered the stoppage of all public works undertaken by the Belgian communes and provinces for the relief of unemployment, that she had already removed to Germany many of the instruments and machines of labor, that the forced labor to which the deportees were condemned was work for the enemy, often on military roads and trenches near the front, that hence the Belgians were willing to suffer punishment and go into exile rather than work, and that many Americans pitied and applauded them. When Mr. Millis describes the staff of the American Legation in Brussels and the American correspondents

either in Wall Street or in Downing Street to explain the American attitude toward the war. Whatever may have been the effect of hired propaganda or the influence of financial and commercial interests, they do not fully account for our intervention.

What really happened, we believe, was that from the very beginning of the war American sympathies were engaged. On top of that, and of decisive importance, the course which the Government took in demanding observance of its traditional neutral rights engaged the national honor of the United States in the defense of the principle that its trade should continue and that its nationals were entitled to protection in the exercise of that trade. When those rights were curtailed by Great Britain, we protested. When our citizens who were exercising those rights were killed by Germany, when our ships

---

as naïve for not emphasizing that Belgian *francs tireurs* were technically guilty of atrocities in sniping at the invading troops and that the German high command was technically justified in lining up local hostages and shooting them, he misses the point; no emphasis on the illegality of the Belgian civilian action or the legality of the German military reprisals would have made the American public of that day feel that the Belgian defenders were not acting heroically and justifiably and that the German invaders were not acting in a contrary sense. Other cases could be cited of failure to appreciate the origins of the sentiment which as the war developed played an important part in shaping American policy. The hostile and criminal acts of German agents in the United States irritated the public much more than Mr. Millis can remember—and were placed in a different category from the propaganda and publicity work of Allied writers and lecturers. It seems to us unrealistic to imagine that deep-rooted sentiment can be dismissed as an important factor in determining the policies of nations; perhaps it is unjustified to assume that its elimination is necessarily desirable, even though one can prove that in specific cases it might well be.

were sunk, and when Germany formally challenged our asserted rights through the unrestricted submarine campaign, then we went to war. If the basic conception of our policy was sound, what other course in self-respect could we have followed?[4] Whether or not the conception was sound is the question to consider.

Upon the outbreak of war we started out with the idea that there must be certain inherent rights of trade, a thesis which we had consistently maintained throughout our history. Like his predecessors—Washington, Adams, Jefferson and Madison —President Wilson was soon engaged in the effort to keep out of war, maintain neutrality, and at the same time make good the illusive and indefinite doctrine known as the Freedom of the Seas. But now there was no serious question of embargoes or nonintercourse as in the days of Jefferson. Trade was too important. To be sure, when Congress met in December 1914, bills were introduced to embargo the export of arms and munitions, one of them sponsored by an influential Democrat, Senator Hitchcock of Nebraska. The influences which prevented its adoption were not primarily commercial. As Mr.

[4] Count Bernstorff, German Ambassador at Washington, in a statement issued to the press immediately after being handed his passports on February 3, 1917, said: "I am not surprised. My government will not be surprised either. The people in Berlin knew what was bound to happen if they took the action they have taken. There was nothing else left for the United States to do." ("War Memoirs of Robert Lansing," p. 217.)

Millis notes, the Hitchcock Bill suffered from being presented as a humanitarian measure rather than as a move to keep us out of the war, and it was attacked (and defeated) as preparing an "unneutral" change in our laws after a foreign conflict had begun. Nevertheless, the fact that our people had never doubted their right and ability to continue trade with belligerents and still remain neutral, and the fact that the relinquishment of that trade would have played havoc with many fundamental American occupations, were root causes of our whole attitude.

As a legal basis for the position which we assumed regarding trade we first tried to make use of the Declaration of London of 1909, which defined contraband, blockade, etc. With all its defects, it would have served as a useful statement of what we then hoped was the international law on the subject. Great Britain, however, had never ratified the Declaration of London and refused to apply it without modifications which we felt deprived it of its real value.[5]

[5] In passing, we may note that the Declaration of London was a treaty solemnly negotiated in the British capital, approved and signed by the British delegates, and accepted by the House of Commons. Due to its rejection by the House of Lords, it was never ratified by the British Government. Thus though it was approved by the United States Senate it of course was never put into effect by the President. The United States is thus not the only power which has failed to ratify the signature of its negotiators to an important treaty.

Lord Grey commented as follows upon the Declaration of London:

Had it been in full force its rules would have hampered us in some respects, particularly in the list of contraband, at the outset of the war; and those who opposed and defeated it are entitled on this account to take credit for their action. Whether, if the Declaration had been ratified and observed as a whole by the belligerents, the balance of advantage and disadvantage would have been in our favor or not is a different question, and one less easy to answer. If it had prevented the submarine war on merchant vessels, it would have saved us from our greatest peril in the war. To this it may be replied that, but for the German submarine war on merchant vessels, the United States would not have come in on the side of the Allies.

The question is not worth pursuing: if the Declaration had been ratified, it would have been broken. The same ruthless spirit that introduced the use of poison-gas, an offense not only against rules of war but against all humane considerations, would have made short work of the Declaration of London.[6]

When the Declaration of London had to be abandoned we fell back upon what we claimed to be the recognized rules of international law. But in doing so we had to recognize that international law failed to give us a definite code and that this failure would "undoubtedly be the source of numerous controversies." [7] Further, particularly in our dealings with the British, the doctrines we had main-

---
[6] Lord Grey, "Twenty-five Years, 1892-1916," v. II, p. 105-6.
[7] "Woodrow Wilson: Life and Letters," v. V, p. 218.

tained in the Civil War came in to plague us. We had ourselves broadened the idea of "continuous voyage," the doctrine under which we seized goods which were en route to a neutral port but which we asserted had an ultimate enemy destination; and we had extended the list of contraband. In writing to Senator Stone on January 20, 1915, Secretary of State Bryan admitted:

The record of the United States in the past is not free from criticism. When neutral, this Government has stood for a restricted list of absolute and conditional contraband. As a belligerent, we have contended for a liberal list, according to our conception of the necessities of the case.

In the same letter, in discussing the trade with neutral ports, Secretary Bryan added:

It will be recalled, however, that American courts have established various rules bearing on these matters. The rule of "continuous voyage" has been not only asserted by American tribunals but extended by them.[8]

But even more serious than these admissions was our recognition in an early communication to Great Britain,

that the commerce between countries which are not belligerents should not be interfered with by those at war unless such interference is manifestly an imperative necessity to protect their national safety, and then only to the extent that it is a necessity.[9]

[8] "Papers Relating to the Foreign Relations of the United States," 1914, Supplement, The World War, p. ix.
[9] Cable of Secretary Bryan to Ambassador Page, December 26, 1914. *ibid.*, p. 373.

It did not take the British long to reach the conclusion that the suppression of our trade with Germany was an imperative necessity. As Lord Grey stated,

> the object of [British] diplomacy, therefore, was to secure the maximum of blockade that could be enforced without a rupture with the United States.

Simultaneously with the interruption of our trade with Germany another phenomenon occurred. Our trade with the Allies grew to a point where it more than took the place of the German trade. Thus the domestic political and economic effect of the British blockade, except in certain limited circles, was not enduring. The international consequences were, however, portentous.

The United States took a position which was logical and which fitted both the sentimental and the national interests of the country, namely that we were under no duty arbitrarily to rectify the consequences of British control of the sea. We would trade where we could, and thus fill the gaps caused by the loss of trade with Germany, whose ports, as well as the ports of neighboring countries, were largely closed to us as a result of the extension of the contraband list and the doctrine of continuous voyage. Further, we considered it objectionable as a matter of principle to change what we conceived to be the rules of neutrality during the course of the war. Thus Secretary Bryan wrote to Count von Bernstorff on April 21, 1915:

... any change in its own laws of neutrality during the progress of a war which would affect unequally the relations of the United States with the nations at war would be an unjustifiable departure from the principles of strict neutrality.[10]

The answer was Germany's submarine challenge to British sea power. In the face of this the legal precedents to which we were clinging seemed more secure. There were no serious Civil War precedents to embarrass us in protesting against the illegalities of submarine warfare, for submarines had not then been invented. Further, in that war the lives of civilians whether on neutral or belligerent merchant vessels had been generally safeguarded, again largely because the submarine was not yet invented.

When, therefore, Germany in February 1915 proclaimed that the waters surrounding Great Britain were to be considered within the seat of war our answer was the "strict accountability" note. We stated in that note that

the Government of the United States would be constrained to hold the Imperial German Government to a strict accountability for such acts of their naval authorities and to take any steps it might be necessary to take to safeguard American lives and property and to secure to American citizens the full enjoyment of their acknowledged rights on the high seas.[11]

[10] "Papers Relating to the Foreign Relations of the United States," 1915, Supplement, The World War, p. 162.
[11] *Ibid.,* p. 99.

There, in a few words, is the thesis which, logically pursued, led to war. It was stated before the blossoming of the "war boom" based on trade with the Allies, and seven months before the first Allied public loan in this country. We were insisting on what we claimed to be full enjoyment of *acknowledged rights*. In a note to Germany a few months later the same idea appears:

> The rights of neutrals in time of war are based upon principle, not upon expediency, and the principles are immutable. It is the duty and obligation of belligerents to find a way to adapt the new circumstances to them.[12]

This might have been Jefferson speaking in 1801. If we meant what we said, war would become inevitable whenever, weighing the advantages and disadvantages of adding us to the list of her enemies, Germany felt impelled to act contrary to these "immutable principles" and "acknowledged rights." True, we had admitted the law of necessity in our earlier notes to Great Britain where trade only was involved; but we did not recognize that the law of necessity could be invoked to justify putting the lives of our citizens in jeopardy. Said Secretary Lansing on June 9, 1915:

> But the sinking of passenger ships involves principles of humanity which throw into the background any special circumstances of detail that may be thought to affect the cases.... The Government of the United States is contending

[12] *Ibid.*, p. 481.

for something much greater than mere rights of property or privileges of commerce. It is contending for nothing less high and sacred than the rights of humanity, which every Government honors itself in respecting and which no Government is justified in resigning on behalf of those under its care and authority.[13]

These grave words, and the acts to which they were the prelude, should be a lesson to us that in the last analysis it is the attack on human life, rather than the attack on property interest, which is most likely to set in motion the tides of resentment which can impel a country like the United States into war. It is more important as a war-prevention measure for us to avoid incidents which might involve the lives of our citizens than to curtail trade relationships, provided it is possible to maintain the latter without risk to American lives.

There is no doubt that President Wilson was just as sincere in his desire to maintain neutrality as President Roosevelt was in 1935. "The United States," he said on August 19, 1914, "must be neutral in fact as well as in name during these days that are to try men's souls. We must be impartial in thought as well as in action, must put a curb upon our sentiments as well as upon every transaction that might be construed as a preference of one party to the struggle before another." [14]

[13] *Ibid.*, p. 437.
[14] The full text of President Wilson's Proclamation of Neutrality, August 4, 1914, and of his Statement of August 19, 1914, is given in Appendix 1 and Appendix 2.

Theodore Roosevelt in September 1914 thought it "eminently desirable" to remain neutral. It was not until some months later that he accused Wilson of "poltroonery" for not having protested the invasion of Belgium. His change of mind is not attributable mainly to political motives, though his love of political invective undoubtedly played a part. What happened to him happened to many other Americans, some sooner, some later. They saw a battle royal in progress, and in their hearts they took sides. Then, as the position which our Government had taken from the very outset produced the material and legal grounds for participation, feeling and fact coalesced; we participated.

Today we must recognize that President Wilson was waging a losing fight. Human beings do not behave as he pleaded with the American people to behave. "A government can be neutral," said Walter Hines Page, "but no *man* can be." [15] Even when war broke out in a region as remote as Ethiopia, the majority of Americans took sides. This was not due to any direct attack on our national interest; and the fact that many of them favored the Ethiopians was certainly not because the Ethiopian propaganda machinery was more active than that of Italy, or because our material interests were bound up in an Ethiopian victory—quite the contrary. The plain fact is that our sentiments will become en-

---

[15] "Life and Letters of Walter Hines Page," v. I, p. 361.

gaged in almost any conflict, especially if it is prolonged and involves general principles in which we are interested. Possibly this shows our naïveté. Possibly it is to our credit. In any event the characteristic is an American one of long standing. We cannot rely for the maintenance of neutrality on the calm and measured judgment of our press and people. Any serious incident which seemed to involve our national honor would find us again ready to fight, despite our devotion to peace in the abstract and despite the activities of peace societies or the churches. What we should plan to do, if our principal desire is to avoid war, is to keep our national honor at home—not let it get tied up with the exercise abroad, in war zones, of any preconceived rights which are not in fact essential to our national existence.

We can admit that this is not a daring policy and that it will not be an easy policy to apply, since as the technique of war develops who can predict how far the belligerents may extend their "war zones," or when or how our national honor or our vital interests may be engaged despite anything we now may do? But at least it is safe to assert that the alternate policy, the attempt to maintain what in the past we have considered our full rights, is not worth the added risk of being caught in war if the world goes mad again.

CHAPTER IV

THE NEUTRALITY ACT OF 1935

THE things which states at war usually seek to acquire abroad may be divided roughly into three categories: the actual arms and implements used in military action; money and credits to buy arms and other supplies; and those multifarious raw materials and manufactured goods which under modern conditions nourish the economy of a nation whether it is at peace or war, furnish the sinews of industry whether it is working for the civilian population or the military, clothe and feed civilians and soldiers alike, and transport them either to the factory or the trenches.

The third category used to be divided into contraband and non-contraband. Certain goods generally recognized under international law as contraband, *i.e.* of direct use in military or naval armaments, were liable to capture if found in transit to the enemy from a neutral. Non-contraband goods were exempt. On the border-line were materials called "conditional contraband," goods liable to seizure if destined for the armed forces. About the contraband list there was always dispute, the neutral trading nation endeavoring to restrict it as much as possible, the blockading belligerent attempting to broaden it. New methods of warfare, involving whole civilian populations and not merely their professional armies, led to such an extension of contraband and conditional contraband that finally in the World War hardly any important article of commerce remained on the free lists of the Allied nations. An American Senator once drily asked whether ostrich feathers had been banned yet. In effect, the term "contraband" had lost much of its meaning. The repeated demands and protests made by the United States to the Allies, based on its alleged right as a neutral to ship to the Central Powers goods which it claimed were non-contraband, remained demands and protests only; the alleged rights remained without recognition from the Allies, and so remain to this day. As many writers have pointed out, in an era when practically everything is contraband the doctrine of the Freedom of the Seas is dead, killed, so far as its application in any major conflict goes, by the action of the Allies in the World War and by our own eventual acquiescence.

There used formerly to be a fourth category of exports from neutral to belligerent states—men. But mercenaries are no longer hired out by avaricious sovereigns, and many nations have laws punishing or at least regulating the entry of their citizens into foreign armies.

How far did the neutrality legislation (S. J. Res. 173) passed by Congress on August 24, 1935, and signed by President Roosevelt on August 31,[1]

[1] Text in Appendix 6.

cover the three categories of exports referred to above? The answer to this question will also indicate whether or not the action of Congress, taken after considerable debate but nevertheless with mixed motives and in an atmosphere of haste, really constituted an effective regulation of all the principal wartime activities of private American citizens which might involve the honor, material interests or sentiments of the American people as a whole. We shall afterwards take up the extension of this legislation made by President Roosevelt at the time of his proclamations of October 5, 1935, and in various important statements thereafter. We shall leave for consideration in a later chapter the question whether the actions taken by the President either by Congressional mandate or on his own authority unjustifiably jeopardized American commercial interests; the relationship of these policies to the effort to preserve world peace by collective action; whether they could be satisfactorily applied in differing circumstances; and hence whether they formed an acceptable precedent for the future.

Section 1 of the Joint Resolution of August 31 prohibited the export of "arms, ammunition, or implements of war" from the United States to any port of a belligerent state, "or to any neutral port for transshipment to, or for the use of, a belligerent country." The President was instructed, "upon the outbreak or during the progress of war between, or among, two or more foreign states," to proclaim the existence of a state of war. He "shall definitely enumerate the arms, ammunition, or implements of war, the export of which is prohibited by this Act."

Both in choosing the moment for proclaiming that a state of war exists, and in the enumeration of prohibited articles, the President was given some discretionary power which is important. Further latitude was contained in the provisions authorizing him from time to time to extend the embargo to states which might become involved in the war as it progressed. The fact that no positive obligation was laid on him to do so might be of great importance in case the League nations should become involved in hostilities as a result of attempting to enforce sanctions against a state which they had declared to be an aggressor.[2]

It should be noted that this particular section of the Act contained a provision that it would expire February 29, 1936. The political causes of this will be discussed later.

In Section 3 a further definite injunction was laid upon the President. Whenever pursuant to Section 1 he has issued a proclamation that a state of war exists, "it shall be unlawful for any American ves-

---

[2] It is also of importance in other situations. Thus it has not yet been suggested that the President should declare that a war exists in China, thereby embargoing the shipment of arms to that country as well as Japan and encouraging Japan to blockade the Chinese coasts.

sel to carry any arms, ammunition, or implements of war to any port of the belligerent countries named in such proclamation as being at war, or to any neutral port for transshipment to, or for the use of, a belligerent country." This supplemented and depended upon Section 1, and thus had only the same span of life, *i.e.* to February 29, 1936.

Further sections (4, 5 and 6) supplemented the President's power to regulate and if need be prevent the shipment from American ports of men, fuel, arms, and other supplies to warships, tenders, and supply ships of a belligerent nation; permitted him to fix the conditions under which submarines of a foreign nation (not necessarily a belligerent) may use American ports and territorial waters, *e.g.* by requiring that they travel on the surface while within our jurisdiction; and permitted him to proclaim that American citizens travelling as passengers on the ships of belligerents do so at their own risk. Enforcement of these provisions was made optional with the President, in the sense that he could determine whether the circumstances required or justified putting them into effect even though a state of war had been found to exist.

The provisions of the 1935 Neutrality Act were mandatory in so far as they related to the prohibition of the export of arms, ammunition and implements of war, the first of the three general categories into which we divided the things which belligerent nations usually seek to buy abroad; the President must see to it that they are not exported, either directly or indirectly, to the nations which he has declared to be at war. It is not clear whether Congress intended that he could withhold application of this provision from nations subsequently entering the war and regarding which he made no declaration. Nor did the Act itself indicate precisely what items were included. However, former treaties signed by the United States which refer to arms and implements of war (including the 1925 Geneva Arms Traffic Convention, ratified June 6, 1935, during the same session of Congress which passed the Neutrality Act) furnished precedents which implied that the list must be narrowly drawn, and certainly drawn to exclude foodstuffs and other raw materials. Senator Pittman, speaking as Chairman of the Foreign Relations Committee during the debate on the bill, said specifically that in his opinion the proposed legislation did not apply to foodstuffs or to raw materials such as cotton.[3] When the Senate voted on August 24 to concur in the House amendments (the most substantial amendment was the one limiting the life of the arms embargo sec-

[3] Senator Fletcher, of Florida: "Mr. President, may I inquire of the Senator whether the articles mentioned—implements of war, and so forth—include such commodities as wheat, corn, cotton, meat, and other food products?" Senator Pittman, of Nevada: "In my opinion, they do not; nor do I believe they do in the opinion of the committee, for the reason that today the definition of arms, ammunition, and implements of war is very generally recognized in international law." *Congressional Record* (daily edition), v. 79, p. 14395.

The Neutrality Act of 1935

tion to approximately six months), only two negative votes were cast, those of Senators Bankhead of Alabama and Gerry of Rhode Island. The other "cotton Senators" and the "wheat Senators" would hardly have been found consenting to the bill without a promise that the staple products of their states were not to be interfered with.

The fact that the oil industry has never been able to line up a powerful group of "oil Senators" to defend its commercial interests has sometimes been alleged to account for the Administration's subsequent emphasis on oil, as compared with cotton and wheat, in plans for maintaining a neutral attitude in the face of the coöperative efforts of European nations to curb Italian aggression. It is a fact that the oil industry is not popular—"oil has a bad smell"—and that there are not great numbers of persons (voters) making their living by it, as in the case of cotton and wheat. But let us be fair. The states belonging to the League of Nations were obviously very likely to decide that a ban on oil exports to a country situated like Italy was the most efficacious single sanction that could be adopted. Further, that embargo would not be open to the same humanitarian objections which might be adduced if foreign nations tried to starve out Italy's civilian population in order to bring pressure on its government. Hence a desire not to be drawn into disputes with all the states participating in collective action might well lead our government to try to keep American oil exports to Italy down to the peace-time level.

The President at first seemed cautious about committing himself as to just what meaning was to be attributed to the words "arms, ammunition and implements of war." Indeed, the descriptive phrase used in the statement which he issued on August 31 when signing the Neutrality Act—"arms, etc."— was taken by some as indicating a wish to reserve liberty of action on a wider category of war materials than would seem to be covered in the limited and explicit phraseology of the Act. This, however, was only guesswork. The official enumeration of embargoed articles issued on October 5 [4] mentioned almost no articles not directly susceptible of military use alone. The list met with no criticism, except perhaps from manufacturers of airplanes and airplane engines who had hoped that models not specifically designed for combat might escape inclusion.

Regarding money and credits for belligerents, the Act was silent. Senator Pittman indicated that this was partly because of the complexity of the problems involved, partly because of the existence of the so-called "Johnson Act" of April 13, 1934, prohibiting loans to governments in default on obligations to the Government of the United States.[5] Speaking in the Senate on August 24, Senator Johnson emphasized that the legislation bearing his name

[4] Text in Appendix 8. [5] Text in Appendix 3.

provided "law enough" to cover effectively all contingencies likely to arise in the course of the impending Italo-Ethiopian crisis. For this reason Congress seemed to think it safe to leave the question of a formal embargo on loans to belligerents for further investigation and action at a subsequent session.

Presumably in order to answer the widespread demand for some control over the activities of munitions makers, and to provide for continuing study of the varied and complex problems involved, the Act also set up (Section 2) a permanent National Munitions Control Board, consisting of the Secretaries of State, the Treasury, War, the Navy and Commerce. All manufacturers, exporters and importers of arms, ammunition and implements of war are required to register with the Board, which shall each year publish the pertinent data which it collects regarding American individuals and firms engaged in the munitions industry and trade. The inclusion of this provision in the Neutrality Act was more or less fortuitous, being due to the public interest lately aroused by the hearings of the Nye Committee on the activities of munitions makers and the trade in arms. It came into effect November 29, 1935, at which time the State Department announced that 86 firms had so far registered with the Board; warning was given that any manufacturers and distributors which did not register after a short period of grace would be prosecuted.

CHAPTER V

WHY CONGRESS ACTED

WHY did Congress turn to the extremely complicated and contentious problems of neutrality at the fag end of an acrimonious session and in torrid summer weather? The reason is not far to seek. Mussolini's menacing attitude toward Ethiopia showed that a war would probably be in progress before Congress reconvened in January 1936, and by common consent the American people wanted nothing to do with it.

Americans have a strong feeling for peace, in the abstract at any rate. But they are vague about what it is and about how to maintain it. They are progressive and scientifically minded and like to think that their approach to the problems of the machine age is realistic. But they have been slow to grasp the transformations which scientific discovery, industrialization and the development of communications have made in society and in international relationships. The feeling of continental security and of aloofness from Europe had been dominant in the United States for so long that when the World War was over the public were predisposed toward accepting the idea that they had blundered into it or been manoeuvred into it, and that they could easily stay out of similar entanglements in the future if only their government would mind its own business and not be enticed into taking part in collective efforts to save the world.

In the spring of 1935, at the unmistakable signs that a new war was being prepared in Africa, and fearing that it might furnish the spark for another European conflagration, the American public were filled with a healthy determination not to become involved in it for reasons that were not clearly understood and deliberately accepted. This determination had recently been augmented by the allegations made and the facts disclosed during the Nye Committee's investigation of the international traffic in arms. The public's feeling still had about it a good deal of the old conception that peace is a state of mind rather than a fluid condition resulting from a continuing series of positive acts, that it is something bestowed rather than something bought at a price. It still reflected the confusion between the ideas of "isolation" and "safety" which had been produced at the time of the fight over whether or not the United States should join the League of Nations. But for some time it had shown signs of becoming more positive and constructive than isolationist sentiment had been in the immediate postwar period, indicating that perhaps the old irreconcilables were passing power to younger, more realistic and more imaginative leaders.

Among the signs pointing in this direction was the fact that President Roosevelt in the autumn of 1932 had carried many states usually considered to be isolationist on a platform which was not afraid to advocate making the Briand-Kellogg Pact more effective "by provisions for consultation and conference in case of threatened violation of treaties." This led naturally enough to the offer of consultation and of at least passive coöperation made by Norman Davis at the Disarmament Conference at Geneva on May 22, 1933, though Mr. Davis was careful to stipulate that his proposal was conditional on the signature of a disarmament treaty.[1] The Disarmament Conference failed; and even earlier debates in the Senate made plain that some Senators considered the Davis proposal unacceptable. Nevertheless, it stood as a harbinger of what President Roosevelt evidently hoped might become a trend in national policy.

In view of the American Government's prominent part in elaborating the Briand-Kellogg Pact,

[1] Mr. Davis's words were as follows: "In addition I wish to make it clear that we are ready not only to do our part toward the substantive reduction of armaments but, if this is effected by general international agreement, we are also prepared to contribute in other ways to the organization of peace. In particular, we are willing to consult with other states in case of a threat to peace, with a view of averting conflict. Further than that, in the event that the states, in conference, determine that a state has been guilty of a breach of the peace in violation of its international obligations and take measures against the violator, then, if we concur in the judgment rendered as to the responsible and guilty party, we will refrain from any action tending to defeat such collective effort which the states may thus make to restore peace." (Press Release, American Delegation, Geneva.)

it was quite natural that the openly avowed intention of a signatory of that treaty to violate its promise not to resort to war should produce an appeal to the United States from the nation about to be attacked. The Emperor of Ethiopia made such an appeal on July 3, 1935. In his reply, Secretary Hull said he was reluctant to believe that any party to the Pact would make war to achieve its national ends, and expressed the hope that "the arbitral agency dealing with this controversy may be able to arrive at a decision satisfactory to both the governments immediately concerned."

There followed a series of interviews between Secretary Hull and the Italian, British and French Ambassadors. On July 12 the Secretary said that the Pact was "no less binding now than when it was entered into by the sixty-three nations that are parties to it," and repeated that "it constitutes a treaty by and among those nations." But apart from an appeal to reason and duty there seemed nothing which the United States could do to ward off the impending war. The Briand-Kellogg Pact, though a treaty, does not require its signatories to take action against a violator. It may give them a legal right to modify their attitude toward that violator; but this is a matter for consideration after war breaks out, by each party individually. Whether or not the United States was likely to take such a stand, the Italian Government evidently discounted the possibility. At least no slackening in Italian preparations for war occurred. On August 1 President Roosevelt issued a statement that he hoped the League of Nations might be able to compose the Italo-Ethiopian dispute. He did not refer to the Pact.

In his final review of the situation, given to the press on September 12, Secretary Hull made this final appeal:

> Armed conflict in any part of the world cannot but have undesirable and adverse effects in every part of the world. All nations have the right to ask that any and all issues, between whatsoever nations, be resolved by pacific means. Every nation has the right to ask that no nations subject it and other nations to the hazards and uncertainties that must inevitably accrue to all from resort to arms by any two.[2]

It remained without effect.

As Mussolini's legions poured through Suez the American people spoke loudly to their representatives at Washington, demanding that they make ready to avoid being caught in any way in the impending hostilities. Several members of Congress already had introduced bills designed to safeguard the neutrality of the United States; and as the threat of war in Africa increased others appeared, some of them quite drastic. From January 10 to August 17, 1935, no less than five so-called neutrality bills were introduced in the Senate, and ten in the House.

[2] Department of State Press Release. For full text of the Statement see Appendix 7.

Some aimed to prohibit loans and credits to belligerents, some proposed arms embargoes, some covered both questions and others besides. The chief rival to the Senate measure which was eventually adopted, and which has been described in a previous chapter, was the Joint Resolution introduced in the House by Mr. McReynolds on August 17, 1935 (H. J. Res. 386). Mr. McReynolds proposed to give the President power to discriminate between belligerents in applying an arms embargo, thus enabling him to act differently toward the victim than toward an aggressor, as well as putting him in a position to facilitate (or rather, avoid opposing) the application of sanctions by the League of Nations. A majority in the Senate were against giving the President this right. The prevailing Senate view was that to allow the President to discriminate between belligerents was tantamount to allowing him to pick the aggressor, which meant taking sides morally. Some Senators thought that this would be a risky procedure. The Senate did not discuss in detail, nor did the public understand, the second question involved, namely, the effect our stand would have on the League's ability to act effectively against an aggressor. The elucidation of that problem was put over until later.

The fact that the McReynolds bill was introduced in the House at the instigation of the Administration showed that the Department of State was afraid of having its hands tied in unforeseen circumstances. There was no objection to the idea of an arms embargo, although in the past, prior to the Chaco war, we had applied it only in instances of internal strife abroad, rather than in cases of international warfare.[3] As far back as 1898 Congress had by Joint Resolution empowered the President to prohibit the export of war material in certain circumstances, and the measure remained in effect until superseded in 1912 by a Joint Resolution (instigated by the turmoil in Mexico), permitting the President to prevent the export of "munitions" to countries on the American continent where there was civil strife. This in turn was extended in 1922 to apply to nations where we enjoyed extraterritorial rights, China being the country chiefly in mind. But the Administration was opposed to the idea that the President should have no freedom of choice about when an embargo should be invoked and about the nations specifically affected; and of course there was even more opposition to the idea that he could not extend the embargo if he thought wise to commodities useful in military operations but not comprised in the limited definition "arms, ammunition and implements of war." The Department of State pointed out that the term "munitions" used in the earlier legislation gave far more latitude, and that no complaint had been heard

[3] For a note on previous American arms embargoes see Appendix 10. Also see "The Embargo Resolutions and Neutrality," by Joseph P. Chamberlain, *International Conciliation,* June, 1929.

on the score that the President had abused his authority.

The Administration's position in this matter was not assumed as a result of snap judgment. As far back as the winter of 1933-1934 the Department of State had come to realize something which had more or less escaped its attention during the administrations of Presidents Harding, Coolidge and Hoover. It realized that although the United States Government had often expressed its concern for world peace and disarmament, and had participated in many arbitration agreements, in regional agreements like the Washington Treaties, and even in a general undertaking like the Pact of Paris, no serious and detailed studies had yet been made with a view to developing a detailed program of action in case the treaty safeguards to world peace should fail, in case war should break out between two or more other nations, and in case the United States suddenly should have to choose (in the light of its experience in the past, and particularly between 1914 and 1917) which of its traditional rights were vital and could and should be defended to the uttermost, and which were untenable and unessential and might be relinquished.

How, for example, had the position of the United States been affected by the new fact that some fifty nations had, by signing the League Covenant, agreed to do away with neutrality as between themselves and an aggressor? Was the Pact of Paris a treaty, conferring rights and duties on its signatories beyond the merely negative duty to refrain from resorting to war as an instrument of policy? Had the new methods and machines of war in the air and under the sea, the new means of communication and propaganda, the developments of science and the consequent alterations in the economic capabilities and needs of various nations, affected vitally the position of the United States as a world power and its ability to remain outside disputes originating on other continents? If so—and the answer seemed obviously to be "yes"—then what program suited to the new conditions should our Government adopt in order to avoid being entangled in futile and dangerous controversies and in order to reserve its full material and moral weight for the support of vital national interests? Certain of these questions had been raised in the important declaration made by Secretary Stimson in addressing the Council on Foreign Relations, on August 8, 1932, but nothing concrete in the way of legislation had been considered. It was indeed high time to begin giving this matter deep and continuing study.

In an article published in *Foreign Affairs* in April 1934 Mr. Charles Warren set out to answer some of the questions involved. Mr. Warren had been Assistant Attorney-General in the Wilson Administration and had wrestled with the legal aspects of the neutrality problem prior to our entry into the

World War. He now drew on his unique experience to list the points where the position of the United States seemed particularly exposed, and where he thought legislation was needed in order to lessen the risk of further embroilment in foreign wars. Mr. Warren did not minimize the price which the American people would have to pay to remain neutral. He was not sanguine that the price might not seem to them too high; and he consequently drew the moral that their first interest and duty should be to reconsider the question of joining with other nations in any practicable step to prevent the occurrence of war, so as to avoid if possible being forced to choose between the horrid alternatives with which the outbreak of war would certainly face them.

Mr. Warren not long afterwards was invited to assist the Department of State in drawing up a program of neutrality legislation to be sponsored by the Administration; and the McReynolds bill and to some degree the Joint Resolution eventually adopted showed the influence of his views. We therefore may summarize the proposals which he put forward in his article as affording a fairly good outline of what thoughtful persons even then realized would have to be done if the United States could hope even to make a reasonable effort to remain at peace. Mr. Warren's proposals were that when war breaks out anywhere the American Government shall:

1. Take over control of all high-power radio stations, and forbid the use of radio instruments by any foreign ship in our ports or waters.

2. Forbid the sale of arms and ammunition to belligerents.

3. Even if all such sales are not prohibited, at least prohibit their shipment in American vessels; further, forbid American citizens to travel as passengers or crew on any ship, belligerent or domestic, carrying arms or munitions.

4. Forbid the entrance into our ports of merchantmen armed either for offense or defense; and forbid American citizens to travel on such ships.

5. Close our ports to any ship of a belligerent nation which permits its ships to fly the American flag for purposes of deception.

6. As a preliminary measure, revise present treaties so as to be free to forbid prize ships from being brought into our ports.

7. Bar American ports and waters to all foreign submarines; and forbid the aircraft of belligerent nations to descend on or pass over American territory.

8. Oblige merchant ships of belligerents in our ports at the outbreak of war to leave within a specified time, on pain of being taken into custody until such time as they desire to clear.

9. Forbid the use of our ports as bases for the supply of food and coal to belligerent warships on the high seas; and in general forbid entrance to our ports and waters of any ship of a belligerent which shall have violated the law

of neutrality or our statute laws, as well as forbid clearance to any ship, domestic or foreign, owned by any corporation or person which shall have committed such a violation.

10. Consider merchant ships chartered or requisitioned by belligerent governments as supply ships of their navies, and intern them if they remain in our waters longer than international law allows for belligerent war vessels.

11. Forbid loans to belligerent governments by private citizens.

12. Forbid not only recruitment for belligerent armies, but also the collection here of foreign reservists; and forbid enlistment of American citizens in the armies of belligerent countries.

Mr. Warren further urged at length that in any future major war the United States should not attempt to insist on alleged neutral rights of trade. "It is better," he wrote, "that our citizens should run the risk of commercial loss than that the country should be involved in a war to protect their alleged commercial rights." And he added that "our Government might very properly say, in effect, to its citizens during the war: you engage in such trade at your own risk during the existence of the war, and you can protect your trade by requiring a profit correlative to the risk."

We may feel sure that in the early spring of 1935 the American public did not realize that if they were to hope to remain neutral in a new World War they would have to do at least all this, and perhaps in addition put such a drastic curb on trade with belligerents that it would in effect amount to non-intercourse. The realization did not come even with the clear approach of hostilities in Africa and the obvious danger that they might spread to Europe. Yet those events did have the effect of making the public call for action which, while not nearly so comprehensive as Mr. Warren suggested, nevertheless started along the road he had mapped out. The result was the legislation of August 31, 1935.

It was the Senate bill which was finally passed. There was considerable debate in both the upper and lower house, and talk even was heard among some of the western Senators about a filibuster to prevent the adjournment of Congress unless the Administration gave way on its demand for discretionary powers. The result represented more of a truce between the Senate and the House (supporting the Administration) than a Senate victory. This was shown by the fact that Section 1 which provided for a mandatory arms embargo, to be applied impartially to belligerents, was adopted only for a six months' period. The battle was left to be fought again at the 1936 session of Congress.

The President's intention to take part in this battle was shown in the comments which he made at the time of signing the Act, especially the protest against "the inflexible provisions of Section 1," which, he said, "might drag us into war instead of keeping us out." And he added, evidently with a broader objection in mind, that "it is the policy of the Government by every peaceful means and without entanglement to coöperate with other similarly minded governments to promote peace."[4]

[4] For text see Appendix 6.

CHAPTER VI

PRESIDENT ROOSEVELT'S INTERPRETATION OF THE ACT

WHEN early in October the Italo-Ethiopian war at last became an uncontrovertible fact,[1] President Roosevelt issued two proclamations to give effect to the wishes of Congress as set forth in the Neutrality Act. Both were dated October 5, 1935. One declared that a state of war existed, admonished the public to observe the provisions of the Act, and enumerated the articles considered arms, ammunition and implements of war.[2] The other (released a day later, on October 6) warned American citizens to abstain from traveling on any vessels of either of the belligerent nations, and added: "I do hereby give notice that any citizen . . . who may travel on such a vessel, contrary to the provisions of the said Joint Resolution, will do so at his own risk." [3]

---

[1] On October 3 a proclamation of the Italian High Commissioner in East Africa stated that he had "given orders for the troops to cross the Mareb" (the frontier of Eritrea and Ethiopia). Other official communiqués of that date spoke of "enemy troops," "the first war flight over Adowa and Adigrat," etc., and the next day reported successful bombings and the capture of certain Ethiopian towns. Speaking some weeks later, on Armistice Day, President Roosevelt referred to his prompt proclamation that hostilities had begun. He said: "We are acting to simplify definitions and facts by calling war 'war' when armed invasion and a resulting killing of human beings take place."

[2] Text in Appendix 8.

[3] Text in Appendix 9.

The President was on vacation at the time, cruising on a battleship in southern waters. But he hastened to make plain that he did not think his duty stopped with invoking the letter of the law. Simultaneously with publishing the first of the above proclamations he issued a statement through the State Department which, after referring to "the situation which has unhappily developed between Ethiopia and Italy," concluded with the following warning: "In these specific circumstances I desire it to be understood that any of our people who voluntarily engage in transactions of any character with either of the belligerents do so at their own risk."

Some observers who knew what a break this announcement made with the past have said that the American public did not comprehend the momentous decision which lay hidden in that one sentence. Probably this was true. The Freedom of the Seas now had disappeared not only in fact, it was gone in name also; American trade with nations at war was no longer (at any rate pending some reversal of policy) to enjoy the protection of the American Government; and this loss of what Jefferson had called "inalienable rights," what Wilson had called "acknowledged rights," had been accepted by the public almost unnoticed and almost without complaint. The reason was twofold. To whatever extent the public did realize the magnitude of the American sacrifice of rights formerly prized, it probably thought that in the abstract the renunciation was wise. For it remembered that the policy which the Administration was now reversing was the policy which had involved the United States in both of the great wars fought in Europe since the achievement of American independence—the Napoleonic Wars and the World War. Above all, for the moment the step cost nothing; there was little or no trade with Ethiopia, and trade with Italy continued unaffected.[4] We may be sure that the public would not have remained so indifferent if (taking a situation like that in 1914) the warships of some power had begun seizing American shipments of cotton and wheat and copper and oil, and if to the protests of our shippers, and of the farmers and miners and factory workers lined up behind them, our Government simply said: "You took the risk. We will not intervene."

The Executive warning sounded on October 5 was to be repeated and amplified during October and November. On October 10, Secretary Hull said:

> The warning given by the President in his proclamation concerning travel on belligerent ships and his general warning that during the war any of our people who voluntarily engage in transactions of any character with either of the belligerents do so at their own risk were based upon the policy and purpose of keeping this country out of war—keeping it from

[4] According to the *New York Times* of October 9, business executives questioned at a meeting of the Export Managers Club of New York the day previous revealed that they were not going to be deterred by the President's warning that trade would be at the trader's own risk.

being drawn into war. It certainly was not intended to encourage transactions with the belligerents.[5]

State Department officials assured newspaper men that this was not designed to support the program of sanctions against Italy then under consideration by the League of Nations. They did not deny, however, that it might be considered as a retort to the objections telegraphed to President Roosevelt on October 7 by a group of indignant New York exporters who saw in the Administration's warning a threat to a possibly lucrative trade in war materials, and even to the continuance of their normal peacetime trade with Italy.

The President was still on the U.S.S. *Houston* in southern waters; but he landed at Charleston on October 23, and the next day was back in Washington conferring with Secretary Hull. Events in Europe had not waited on his coming. On the contrary, the League of Nations had been exceedingly busy discussing how to restrain Italian aggression, and had come with unexpected speed to unexpectedly vigorous decisions.

On October 7, the same day that news of the President's first proclamation became known in Geneva, and the day Italy announced the fall of Adowa, the League Council had accepted the report of its "Committee of Six" which pronounced the following unprecedented verdict: "The Italian Gov-

[5] Department of State Press Release.

ernment has resorted to war in disregard of its covenants under Article XII of the Covenant of the League of Nations." On October 10 the Assembly of the League had ratified the verdict. On October 11 the "Committee of Coördination" of the Assembly had moved to apply sanctions by imposing an arms embargo against Italy, utilizing for the purpose the same list of arms, ammunition and implements of war which President Roosevelt had used; and simultaneously League states which had prohibited or restricted the export of arms to Ethiopia had agreed to annul such measures.[6] On October 14 the same Committee had proposed to cut off loans and credits to Italy. By October 19 agreement had been reached on a broad boycott of Italian exports, on an embargo on the shipment to Italy of a number of key war materials, and on other measures aimed at bringing Italy to an observance of the promises it had made in the League Covenant (and incidentally in the Briand-Kellogg Pact).

In the United States a development of importance had begun also to attract attention. On October 8 a news item from Washington noted that for about two months the Italian port of Massaua, in Eritrea, had been the chief importing point in the world for American motor trucks. The appearance of this item happened to synchronize with publication of several

[6] President Roosevelt under the terms of the Neutrality Act had no power to discriminate between the belligerents.

accounts from American correspondents in Eritrea detailing the achievements of Italian road building and describing the progress of the Italian Army via truck. A few days later (October 19) the Commerce Department disclosed that the United States had been supplying a major part of Italy's increased foreign purchases of many products used in making munitions, including cotton waste, iron and steel scrap, copper, benzol, and various chemicals.[7]

These various developments presented the American Government with two alternatives: (1) The Administration could wait until Geneva actually set in operation a system of sanctions, which obviously was bound to include an embargo by the League powers on many goods which were also being shipped from the United States to Italy. In that event, and if the League tried to reinforce sanctions with a blockade, the American Government would have either to bow to League pressure or to condone exploitation by American traders of the efforts being made by European nations to preserve peace and live up to their treaty obligations. There would be the added risk in the offing, moreover, that American commercial interests might become so enamored of a lucrative war trade that they would demand diplomatic protection and (strengthened by the fact of American unemployment) might eventually involve us in dangerous disputes with the League

[7] *New York Times,* October 20, 1935.

powers. Or (2), the Administration might presume that the American people's interest in peace was so intense that it would support any move calculated to prevent the United States from being put in the uncomfortable position of thwarting Europe's collective action for peace, and which at the same time promised to diminish the risk of its own involvement.

The President's statement of October 5 showed that from the start he inclined toward the second course. His feeling apparently became stronger as the League program took shape, though it was repeatedly stated very explicitly on his behalf that he was not actuated by any feeling of obligation toward the League or under the influence of any pledge or any understanding of any description with Great Britain or any other power. Doubtless he was encouraged by the fact that several western Senators, among them as redoubtable an isolationist as Senator Borah, seemed tacitly to approve what he was trying to do. They protested that there must not be coördination of policy between the United States and the League. On the other hand, they did not seem ready to let their inveterate mistrust of the League carry them quite to the point of risking a fight with all the League powers in order to trade with an aggressor designated at Geneva. They did not reveal whether or not they would approve if the Administration chose not to consider the League powers as belligerents in case Geneva's effort to curb Italy led to hostilities. But for the time being no decision on that point was necessary.

In a radio warning on October 7 against the "subtle ways of propagandists," Senator Borah of Idaho, ranking Republican member of the Foreign Relations Committee of the Senate and often mentioned as a possible Republican candidate for the Presidency, demanded that we "courageously remain aloof" from a war "over issues distinctly and every phase of them European." He pointed out that the cost in trade and profits was not to be compared with the cost of becoming involved.[8]

Senator Nye of North Dakota (Republican), on October 11 lent general support to the idea of restricting trade with the belligerents. He attacked the New York shippers who had criticized the President's action under the Neutrality Act. Their "insatiable appetite," he said, would, if given free rein, "lead 138,000,000 people into a war that is none of our business." And he added: "Where commerce and business conflict with neutrality, commerce must be tossed overboard."[9] And on October 16 he telegraphed Secretary Hull his congratulations on "the spirit in which the neutrality policy laid down by Congress just before adjournment is being invoked in the face of pressure all must know to exist."[10]

[8] *New York Times,* October 8, 1935.
[9] *New York Times,* October 12, 1935.
[10] *New York Times,* October 17, 1935.

Senator Vandenberg of Michigan, a member of the Foreign Relations Committee of the Senate and potential Republican candidate for the Presidency, said on October 15: "I am in complete agreement with the new, mandatory American neutrality policy as ordered by Congress and proclaimed by the President. If anything, I would make it more emphatic. It may deny us an expression of our natural sympathies in a given dispute, but it substantially insulates us against dreadful consequences which otherwise could embroil us again in alien wars. The loss of incidental commerce is infinitely less important than the maintenance of American peace. There seems to be an unfortunate disposition in some quarters to link our new neutrality formula with League of Nations sanctions. That was not the Congressional purpose and is not my conception of our formula." [11]

Senator Elbert D. Thomas of Utah, a Democratic member of the Senate Foreign Relations Committee, was reported to have said on November 23 that the new neutrality policy was threatened by American shippers who "wink at the law" by engaging in profitable trade in war sinews with Italy and Ethiopia. The report did not say whether by "the law" he meant the letter of the Neutrality Act or the President's interpretation of its spirit. But the implication was that he referred to the latter.[12]

[11] *New York Times,* October 16, 1935.
[12] *New York Herald Tribune,* November 24, 1935.

On November 28 Senator Borah elaborated his views in a prepared statement. He said that he understood that the Government was acting "wholly apart from the League," but he said he thought it "very reasonable" for us to seek "to hold our exports down to a normal peace basis" as a means of "manifesting our purpose not to take advantage of the war to make war profits." In giving out the statement, he remarked: "I want to help the Government pursue its general course." [13]

An appeal never again to countenance war profits was made by Senator Bennett Champ Clark, Democrat, of Missouri, in the December issue of *Harpers*. Calling the 1935 Neutrality Act a "stop gap," he said that food, clothing, lumber, leather and chemicals are all as important aids in winning a war as are munitions, and made plain that he would favor new legislation placing an embargo on the export of all of them.

Senator Vandenberg in a radio talk on December 19 again called for a neutrality program "unrelated to the League of Nations." The American people must, he said, "make no loans; grant no credits; ship no arms, ammunition or implements of war to *any* belligerent." "We should prohibit American travel on belligerent ships," he said; and added: "In the field of general commodities the prospect is less clear. But a quota system, confining commerce

[13] *New York Times*, November 29, 1935.

to a peace-time rate, or a 'cash and carry' system, making deliveries at our own seaboard, may well offer a basis for solution." Finally, he said "we must make our neutrality legislation mandatory." [14]

But already in October, long before the last of these statements had appeared, the Administration had thought it necessary to intensify its effort to prevent American traders from seeking what was frequently referred to in the Washington dispatches as "blood money." Passing beyond the original warning that American traders could not expect to receive government support if they got into trouble over shipments of goods to warring nations, the State Department adopted the position that such trade should definitely be discouraged and restricted.

On October 30 (three days before the League fixed on November 18 as the date for starting sanctions against Italy, but when Geneva dispatches already indicated that a date was about to be set), the President issued a statement in which he made clear that he favored restricting exports to belligerents to the average of such sales in normal times. He said in part:

> This Government is determined not to become involved in the controversy and is anxious for the restoration and maintenance of peace.
> However, in the course of war, tempting trade opportunities may be offered to our people to supply materials which

[14] Press release of the Columbia Broadcasting System.

would prolong the war. I do not believe that the American people will wish for abnormally increased profits that temporarily might be secured by greatly extending our trade in such materials; nor would they wish the struggles on the battlefield to be prolonged because of profits accruing to a comparatively small number of American citizens.

Accordingly, the American Government is keeping informed as to all shipments consigned for export to both belligerents.

Simultaneously Secretary Hull said that he wished to

reiterate and call special attention to the definite implications and the effect of the policy of this Government to discourage dealings with the two belligerent nations as set forth in the President's public statement of October 5 and my statement of October 10 warning our people not to trade with the belligerents except at their own risk.

And he added a strong argument that "an early peace, with the restoration of normal business and normal business profits, is far sounder and far preferable to temporary and risky war profits." [15]

The statements by the President and Secretary of State were in the nature of a threat. How it might be carried out was not revealed. But the public before long was given the detailed information which evidently had provoked the President and Secretary of State into taking so decided a stand. On November 5 the Department of Commerce announced that American shipments of oil to Italy had

[15] Department of State Press Release.

been 600 percent larger in August and September 1935 than in the same two months the year previous. Further, when the export figures for October came to hand [16] they showed important increases in the amounts sent to Italy of what might be called "war sinews." Total exports to Italy had increased in value only from $6,184,491 in October 1934 to $6,821,366 in October 1935. Italy was cutting down on materials not useful in war, in order to conserve exchange. The categories in which marked increases occurred were significant. Non-metallic minerals (the category including oil) had increased from $382,821 to $1,104,764. Metals and manufactures (except machinery and vehicles) had increased from $502,030 to $1,073,395. Machinery, vehicles and chemicals also showed increases. The increase in exports to Italian Africa was even more striking. The total exports increased from $45,266 in October 1934 to $367,785 in October 1935, almost the whole of the increase being in oil, machinery, vehicles and chemicals. Incidentally there was no increase in the exports of cotton to Italy or to Italian Africa, either in the month of October or in the ten-month period ending with October.

Evidently worried by this growing trade with a warring nation, Secretary Hull on November 15 referred with emphatic disapproval to the shipment of what he termed "essential war materials." He

---

[16] Department of Commerce news release, November 23, 1935.

mentioned by name oil, copper, trucks, tractors, scrap iron and scrap steel. "This class of trade," he said, "although not actually 'arms, ammunition or implements of war,'" is "directly contrary to the policy of this Government as announced in official statements of the President and the Secretary of State, as it is also contrary to the general spirit of the recent Neutrality Act." He added that the Administration was "closely observing the trend and volume of exports" to the two belligerent countries. In the effort to reinforce moral suasion, the Department of Commerce on November 23 sent out letters to American shipping concerns calling the attention of owners and operators of ships under mortgage to the Government that "the carrying of essential war materials such as those mentioned in the statement of the Secretary of State, November 15, destined for either of the belligerents is distinctly contrary to the policy of the Government." It was estimated that the Government had about $97,000,000 outstanding in ship construction loans, and a large amount more due on vessels purchased by various companies.

It was about at this point that some concern began to be felt in Washington lest in its determination not to interfere with or be entangled in a League system of sanctions the Administration might have gone further than necessitated by any actual developments in Europe. The proposal to widen the embargo on raw materials for Italy had gained backing at Geneva, and it was reported that oil, coal, copper and steel might all be added to the list. On November 30 the "Committee of Eighteen" was called for December 12 to consider extending the sanctions against Italy to include oil. Geneva dispatches mentioned that in the discussion of all these proposals the Hull list of November 15 figured prominently. The State Department professed not to be worried by this fact. The declaration was repeatedly made that the neutrality policy of the Administration had been adopted to keep the country out of involvement in the African war, that no pressure from those greedy for war profits would swerve it from its goal, and that it would follow the course it had chosen regardless of what other countries or the League of Nations might do.

The November figures for American exports to the warring nations [17] further substantiated the Washington statement that in certain respects our trade was profiting from the war in Africa. In November 1934 total exports to Italy were valued at $8,418,608; in November 1935 the value was $9,054,915. Non-metallic minerals (including oil) increased from $497,565 to $1,304,722. Metals and manufactures (except machinery and vehicles) rose from $872,071 to $2,026,622. Machinery and vehicles rose from $466,331 to $1,187,383. These

[17] Department of Commerce news release, December 21, 1935.

were the chief increases. Exports of cotton fell. The total exports to Italian Africa rose from $17,971 in October 1934 to $583,735 in October 1935. Exports to Ethiopia remained negligible.

Meanwhile in Europe there seemed to come a realization that the Neutrality Act as passed by Congress, though a welcome aid to the League in trying to deal with the war in Ethiopia, might turn out to be a two-edged sword. As Harold Callender cabled to the *New York Times* from London on December 4:

> It cuts away the once formidable obstacle to a collective blockade, the freedom of the seas policy of the United States. It hits Italy harder than Ethiopia and so reinforces League sanctions. But in a future war it might penalize the nations applying sanctions instead of penalizing the aggressor, and its adverse effect might be most keenly felt by the nation best able to control the seas—that is, Britain.

As to the President's elaboration of the policy laid down by Congress, namely the attempt to discourage all "abnormal" trade with a belligerent, there apparently was even more apprehension, especially in London. Might not the arguments which the Administration had been using commend themselves so strongly to the American public that Congress at its next session would translate the Roosevelt policy into mandatory law, with the result (for instance) that in a war between Great Britain and Germany the United States would be unable to provision the British Isles even though its sympathies might be strongly with a democracy and against a dictatorship, and even though the British fleet was in command of the seas? As Mr. Callender pointed out, whether a nation was fighting in self-defense or for conquest, it would be deprived of access to American supplies. The same fear found expression in the United States from observers like Walter Lippmann.[18]

There is no ground for believing that the transformation which suddenly came over British policy in the second week of December had anything to do with these considerations, nor with the circumstance that American exports of certain war materials to Italy had increased. The general position taken by the United States Government was, in fact, one which could not be construed as standing in the way of effective League action. The warning that American war trade with the belligerents did not have the approval and would not have the support of the Government tended to remove the risk that a League blockade of Italy might involve the League powers in disputes with the United States. As at some stages in the Manchurian affair, our independent course had taken us further—in some respects at any rate—than the League nations had felt able to go.

[18] *New York Herald Tribune,* December 5 and 7, 1935.

Sir Samuel Hoare's reasons for turning about in his tracks probably lay in an entirely different set of circumstances: among others, the fact that one bluff had met another and the bluff of the more reckless and desperate bluffer had prevailed; the fact that to whatever extent British policy had been determined by electoral considerations, those had now been removed; the fact that the French Government was sadly divided, that French eyes were, as always, fixed chiefly on the menace from across the Rhine, and that the *Croix de Feu* and other reactionary organizations strongly opposed vigorous measures against the Italian dictatorship; the fact that Mussolini's friends could always play the trump card of all the fascist dictatorships—the claim that they stood between "civilization" (to use a perhaps inappropriate word) and chaos; the fact that the efficacy of Italian aircraft and submarines against the British fleet in the Mediterranean could not be known definitely without a trial.

It is not for Americans, who would not have to do the fighting if Mussolini resorted to desperate steps as he saw the ring of sanctionist states closing in, to comment on the foregoing reasons and the others which might be cited to explain Sir Samuel Hoare's *volte face*. Neither need we consider here the force of outraged British public opinion which produced Sir Samuel's resignation on December 18. We see that the sentiment for peace and for coöperative action to maintain peace was powerful enough in Great Britain and in other parts of Europe to defeat the program of two strong governments to sacrifice the League of Nations in order to satisfy the appetites of a third great European government. It is sufficient for Americans in studying the neutrality policy of the United States in its relation to those dramatic events if they can feel sure that at no point in the autumn of 1935 did American policy force Great Britain, France and the other chief executors of the League to hold back from acting as vigorously as they wished to maintain the sanctity of international agreements and restore peace.

CHAPTER VII

OUR FUTURE NEUTRALITY POLICY

1. *Basic Neutrality*

WHATEVER neutrality legislation we have already adopted or may adopt cannot possibly be more than a framework, raised in the air, to support the specific policy which, in contingencies yet unrevealed, best promises at a moment of crisis to keep us out of war. Our action in each case will have to be determined in the light of the specific circumstances. All that can be done in advance is to set up certain simple rules which in any event cannot damage us, and which we hope may help the government to deal prudently with each case as it arises.

For example, in a war between states which are not powerful on the seas we may well find it possible to maintain a neutral position without any great interruption of normal American trade. When we proclaimed an arms embargo in the recent war between Paraguay and Bolivia our purpose was to help stop the war, not to avoid any threatened trouble to ourselves. On the other hand, if there is a war in Europe, particularly if England is involved, or in the Far East, with Japan possibly blockading China, we should have great difficulty in avoiding dangerous disputes even if we pressed our renunciation of trade to the utmost limit that the American people would tolerate. Consistency, in other words, is not essential or even possible. And the idea that at the present moment we can be wise and farsighted enough to embody in rigid law the policy which we could consistently follow in varying and even opposite circumstances is positively dangerous.

This prompts the suggestion that it might be wise to divide our neutrality legislation into two categories: basic and supplementary. The first would enumerate the steps which the Executive would be required to take whenever he proclaimed the existence of war in any part of the globe. The second would permit extraordinary safeguards to be taken if the war should vitally affect our safety. It is not suggested that the legislation for the latter contingency should permit discrimination between belligerents—another subject to be discussed presently—but that when the safety and the best interests of the country require special action our legislative framework should permit the choice of the steps best calculated to meet the particular emergency.

There is already in existence a basic neutrality law, largely dating from 1818, invoked at the beginning of the World War, and belatedly supplemented in June 1917 [1]—after we were no longer neutral! This law provides against the use of our territory

[1] See Appendix 4 for the basic neutrality law as of January 3, 1935.

as a base for organized operations by one belligerent against another. Recruiting, fitting out of military expeditions, supplying belligerent vessels on the high seas, and the like, are made criminal offenses. Supplementing this basic law is the Act of August 31, 1935, already described in Chapter III. The only part of this Act which was of a permanent character and which also spoke in mandatory terms was the section relating to the licensing of arms manufacturers and exporters (and this really has no logical place in neutrality legislation, as it applies in time of peace). The life of the mandatory provision against the export of arms was limited to the period until February 29, 1936. The other provisions of the Act, while permanent in character, gave the President discretionary power so that he might act when, in his judgment, action would serve to maintain peace with foreign nations, protect the commercial interests of the United States, or promote its security. When these powers are invoked they apply to all belligerents.[2]

2. *Travel in War Zones*

The most important of the permanent features of the August 1935 legislation was that limiting travel on belligerent vessels. Let us hope that this

[2] We have not endeavored to deal with the complicated aspects of our neutrality policy arising out of our new relations with the Philippine Islands. It is interesting to note that in referring to its territorial scope, the Neutrality Act specifically includes the Philippines among "the insular possessions of the United States."

will long remain on the statute books with very little change. The chief purpose of the provision, "to protect the lives of American citizens," recognized that loss of American lives through the action of a belligerent is the event most likely to jeopardize the maintenance of our neutrality.

Today we can only speculate what would have been the result of such a provision if it had been in effect in 1915. Would it have deterred travel on a ship like the *Lusitania?* Would the popular reaction have been the same if, despite such a warning, loss of life had resulted? Certainly the diplomatic correspondence which started with the *Lusitania* note would have been pursued in a different tone. When in May 1915 the Germany Embassy published its warning[3] against travel on Allied vessels sailing for the war zone, it was generally interpreted as "an impertinent effort" to prevent American citizens from the exercise of their "acknowledged rights." Secretary Bryan did not agree. He had continually advocated warning American citizens against travel on belligerent vessels or vessels carrying cargoes of

---

[3] "NOTICE! Travellers intending to embark on the Atlantic voyage are reminded that a state of war exists between Germany and her allies and Great Britain and her allies; that the zone of war includes the waters adjacent to the British Isles; that in accordance with formal notice given by the Imperial German Government, vessels flying the flag of Great Britain or of any of her allies, are liable to destruction in those waters and that travellers sailing in the war zone on ships of Great Britain or her allies do so at their own risk. IMPERIAL GERMAN EMBASSY, Washington, D. C., April 22, 1915." (From the *Sun*, New York, May 1, 1915.)

ammunition, and his failure to bring Wilson to his point of view on this matter was one of the main reasons for his resignation at the time of the *Lusitania* crisis. It is interesting to note in how many respects the Bryan neutrality policy seems to commend itself to public opinion today. He was viewing the problem, as the American public now does, more from the standpoint of maintaining peace than asserting or preserving alleged neutral rights.

To lessen as much as possible the likelihood of American lives being lost at sea, Congress might broaden the President's authority to warn citizens that travel on belligerent vessels was at their own risk. The words of the 1935 Act could be construed as covering only passengers. The warning might well be made to cover American seamen shipping on belligerent vessels, and possibly, in an extreme case, even travel on American vessels leaving for a war zone, whether as passenger or member of the crew.

3. *The Arms Embargo*

The arms embargo section of the Neutrality Act was not enacted as a permanent measure; but the prevailing sentiment of the country makes it likely that some such embargo, permanent and possibly mandatory in nature, will be a feature of any Act adopted by Congress. We should consider in advance the various effects of such legislation.

The public thinks of arms as falling in a different category, sentimentally and morally, from other materials purchased abroad by belligerents. This is understandable. We all look back on wartime wheat at $3.45 a bushel and wartime cotton at 38 cents a pound with less distaste than we recall the 200 percent stock dividend of the Bethlehem Steel Corporation in January 1917. But actually there is no very strong practical reason for making this differentiation; food and clothing are as necessary to an army as guns. Moreover, the arms embargo may have its dangers unless it is applied in coöperation with the other neutral countries which manufacture arms.[4] The inconvenience would be particularly noticeable in dealing with emergencies in South America, as the existence of mandatory legislation would deprive us of a useful negotiating weapon with which to secure the coöperation of European suppliers of arms.

[4] It is significant that from 90 to 95 percent of the international trade in arms is concentrated in the hands of eight exporting countries, and that only about ten percent of the total is American. The following table (from "Sanctions," Information Department Paper No. 17, Royal Institute of International Affairs) shows the national percentages of the principal exporters:

	1930	1932
Great Britain	30.8	30.1
France	12.9	27.9
United States	11.7	8.7
Czechoslovakia	9.6	4.2
Sweden	7.8	11.0
Italy	6.8	1.7
The Netherlands	5.4	6.2
Belgium	4.4	4.4
	89.4	94.2

Further, the fact that the legislation was in existence, ready for instant use, would likely mean that countries which have no munitions industries of their own and which normally might buy from us, would either feel forced to build factories or would lay plans to secure their armaments from countries other than the United States. The latter consideration may not be important. But it would not be in accordance with our general aims if the embargo led to a broad increase in armaments rather than a decrease. In this connection, it is of more than passing interest to recall that if the habit of promptly laying down an arms embargo impartially against all belligerents had prevailed at the time of the Revolutionary War, the effect on the fortunes of our struggling young nation might have been disastrous. Even today there may be occasions when a general arms embargo would work to benefit the strong nation, well prepared for war, as against a nation which was more peace-loving and less thoroughly prepared.[5]

Those and other objections would be met if the time of applying the arms embargo were left in the President's discretion, subject to his judgment whether in a given situation it would promote the interests of the United States and serve to maintain peace with foreign nations. Presumably the em-

---

[5] For a note on previous American embargoes on arms shipments to belligerents see Appendix 10.

bargo would generally be imposed in accordance with popular wishes; but the President should have the right to withhold it from operation when it would work injustice, or when the failure of other neutral arms manufacturing countries to coöperate nullified its effectiveness. We should not like to see the course of a war in South America determined by the governments which could control the activities of a Vickers-Armstrong, a Schneider-Creusot or a Krupp; and we ought not obligate ourselves to take action which would make that a possibility.

As was often pointed out during the World War, there is nothing in international law which calls upon a neutral to prevent the export of arms to belligerents. No nation, we believe, has bound itself in advance to do so unreservedly and in all cases. We doubt whether the United States should in advance give up all liberty of action in some future war— say, in South America or the Far East—and so risk finding itself unable to negotiate with other neutral nations to help bring the war to a close. American raw materials might play a preponderant role in a war between the great European powers; but arms would be the decisive factor in a struggle between non-industrial states (including most of the countries of this hemisphere), or when one of the contestants was not industrial. "The Joint Resolution," said Senator Hiram Johnson in the Senate on August 24, "makes plain the policy of the United

States of America to keep out of European controversies, European wars, and European difficulties." Did the California Senator forget for a moment the Far East, and the possible effects there of the policy he was approving so strongly for Europe? Senator Connally, though not from a state touching the Pacific, saw other issues involved. He spoke on the same day of the danger of putting the American Government into a "plaster cast," and asked if we were really prepared to refuse arms to Mexico in case a foreign power attacked her, or if we would help isolate Canada if she were attacked.

Before we adopt an automatic arms embargo we ought to see clearly the end of the road.

4. *Loans and Credits*

The so-called Johnson Act, passed April 13, 1934,[6] bans the flotations of further loans in this country (except refunding loans and possibly the borrowing involved in ordinary banking and commercial transactions) by governments or government agencies which are not paying interest on their debts to the Government of the United States. This eliminates the major European powers as potential borrowers. Japan is not among the nations thus excluded from the American financial market; nor does the Act cut off the private industrial companies

[6] Text in Appendix 3.

or munition factories in the countries which are excluded.

The debates which took place at the time the Johnson Act was adopted give ground for believing that in a sense it was an act of vengeance. If the Government now proposes to include foreign loans and credits in its neutrality legislation we believe that this should be accomplished by a separate act and without relation to the war debt situation or the Johnson Act.

Ray Stannard Baker has reminded us how perplexing this problem of loans and credits was during the World War.[7] At the outset Secretary Bryan opposed loans to the belligerents, holding that money was "the worst of all contrabands because it commands everything else." He felt that the powerful financial interests which would be connected with loans would use their influence through the press and otherwise to support the governments whose loans they had floated. Mr. Lansing, then Counsellor of the State Department, supported Secretary Bryan's view that it was wise to discourage "the money of this country from taking part in a foreign war." Consequently, on August 15, 1914, Messrs. J. P. Morgan & Co. were advised that in the judgment of the Government "loans by American bankers to any foreign nation which is at war are inconsistent with the true spirit of neutrality." There

[7] "Life and Letters of Woodrow Wilson," v. V, p. 175 *et seq.*

was, of course, no legal ban on loans; but the statement of government policy was sufficient to prevent their flotation at that time.

A little more than a year was enough to bring about an entire change in this policy. Principles and theories, correct in the abstract, gave way to the hard reality that American trade with the Allies was increasing and that to hold that trade we had to finance it from the moment the credit balance of the Allies on this side of the Atlantic was exhausted. The first breach in the policy related to commercial credits as distinct from what were then called "general loans," that is, loans floated for sale to the general public. Before the end of 1914, inquiring bankers were advised that the warning against loans did not apply to ordinary credit facilities for the shipment of goods to belligerents; and somewhat later (March 31, 1915) this policy was elaborated in an announcement by the State Department. In his letter to Senator Stone, dated January 20, 1915, Secretary Bryan, with the approval of President Wilson, defended this differentiation between public and private loans on the ground that private commercial transactions did not arouse any "general spirit of partisanship."[8] Public loans were still discouraged on the ground that they "would be taken up chiefly by those who are in sympathy with the

[8] "Foreign Relations of the United States," 1914, Supplement, p. xii.

belligerent seeking the loan," and that "the people would be divided into groups of partisans, which would result in intense bitterness and might cause an undesirable, if not a serious, situation." The chart of American industrial activity in the period since 1854, prepared by Colonel Leonard Ayres, shows that there was a severe depression in the United States from the outbreak of the World War until about halfway through 1915. But by August 1915 the flood of Allied buying orders in the United States had reached a point where the rising trend had carried business from below "normal" up into the "prosperity" zone. Private banking credits were no longer adequate; and it became a question either of cutting down on the orders, and facing the economic difficulties which would result, or lifting the ban on loans. The ban was lifted. In September 1915 the first great Anglo-French loan was publicly offered in the United States.[9]

We have here an illuminating example of what would be the likely trend of events in any great foreign war. It is easy to state the theory that we should separate ourselves entirely from the rest of the world if the world goes to war. But when the economic results of such a policy become apparent the pressure to reverse it becomes very strong. To say this is not to imply that there was or would be

[9] See the letter from Secretary Lansing to President Wilson, reprinted in the *New York Times,* August 19, 1935.

any deep-dyed plot of American bankers. What happened in 1915 was an ordinary case of the working of economic law once an abnormal wartime trade had been allowed to develop.

If we are starting out to build up a system of protective neutrality, we should do what we can in advance to head off this trend. To buy the bonds of a belligerent is to gamble on his success; the psychological results may be bad; and the effect on the financial condition of the country in the future may be bad through stimulating mushroom wartime industries. At the present time, any public loan of a foreign government or its agencies floated for the purpose of securing new capital would require registration under our Securities Act; and if it were listed on any registered exchange it also would have to be registered under the Securities Exchange Act. While registration does not imply governmental approval of a loan, it does bring the authorities of the United States into contact with the transaction in question. This might prove embarrassing in the event a belligerent applied for a loan to American bankers. It is therefore suggested that any loan transactions by a belligerent which called for registration under the Securities Act should be banned. Other financial transactions, which presumably would be in the nature of commercial banking credits or private loans, would be permitted in so far as they were only the normal facilities extended to that part of our trade which under other provisions of our neutrality law was allowed to continue. Any undue extension of banking credit to cover trade with belligerents could be controlled to a considerable extent by the Federal Reserve Board.

CHAPTER VIII

TRADE AND PEACE

1. *A Mandatory Embargo on Trade*

WE must also decide what to do about our wartime trade in the broad category of manufactured goods and raw materials—machines, metals, oil, cotton, foodstuffs—which have important uses in war but which are also the mainstays of our peacetime commerce. There has been talk, both in Congress and out, of a mandatory embargo on all such materials, or on certain selected materials.[1] It is to be hoped that no such mandatory legislation will be adopted.

The American people may be ready to accept sacrifices of trade and profits where to continue trade would be to risk war. Certainly they should be. But they would not long tolerate a sweeping prohibition applied indiscriminately in situations where its necessity was not obvious. Many cases are conceivable in which a blanket embargo, crippling to our commerce and adding to unemployment, would not serve any directly useful purpose. Often, too, it might work injustice, as countries which had armed themselves to the teeth and which possessed

---

[1] By mandatory we understand is meant an embargo which would be automatically applied, whenever a state of war has been declared to exist, against all trade in the particular articles banned, destined directly or indirectly for any of the belligerents.

raw materials and industries would automatically be given a decisive advantage over countries less well prepared and less well endowed by nature. Foreign countries, faced with the prospect of sweeping embargo measures by the United States, would accelerate their present efforts to become completely self-sufficient, to the detriment of our remaining export trade and to the added confusion of international commercial relations generally. And perhaps on some future occasion when we ourselves were at war we might find the embargo weapon which we had devised turned against us; for, strong as we feel, we still lack certain materials necessary for our defense.

As the United States has no monopoly of materials useful in war (except perhaps, helium, not a material of major importance), an embargo on our exports would in certain circumstances merely divert our normal trade to our competitors. Oil is the only commodity useful in war of which our production exceeds 50 percent of the total world production; and there is plenty of oil outside the United States —in Russia, Rumania, Mexico, Venezuela and the Middle East—to support the activities of belligerents in major wars. In addition, certain great industrial countries which have little or no oil production at home are trying, regardless of expense, to arrange to have the oil needed in war by extracting it from coal. As for copper, iron, cotton, and a long list of other key war materials, the supply outside the United States is ample.[2]

Hence in many cases an embargo on American exports to belligerents might mean that other nations would profit at our expense. Our producers and traders should be ready to make the sacrifice in a menacing situation where an embargo promised a measure of protection. The difficulty about stating the embargo in mandatory terms is that it then must be invoked in every war, whether or not there seems any risk that without it the United States might become involved in hostilities. If Americans are asked to make needless sacrifices they will protest and revolt; and the difficulty and unpopularity of enforcing the law in such situations will weaken the moral conception on which it is based and make enforcement still more difficult when it is really needed.

One way of demonstrating the inherent difficulty of laying down a mandatory embargo policy is to imagine what it would mean in certain possible war situations, in the event that the same policy were not adopted by the other neutral trading nations.

Imagine, first, a war involving only countries in South America, Central America or the Caribbean area. Such a war would not directly menace the United States, *i.e.* there would be little or no risk

[2] See Appendix II for an analysis, by nations, of the world production of strategic war materials.

that we would ourselves become involved. In that kind of war, the materials needed by the belligerents would be obtained largely from Europe if the United States reservoir were closed. The European countries supplying them would thereby be in a position to influence the outcome of the war, that is to say, control the destinies of countries on this Continent. For as we suggested above in discussing the arms embargo, the possibility of access to foreign markets is a controlling factor in a war waged by non-industrial countries.

Second, take a war in the Far East. Here the possibility of our entanglement is not to be dismissed; and in some circumstances an embargo might be wise, provided it were invoked in concert with the other principal neutral powers. In a Sino-Japanese war, Japan would be the beneficiary of any automatic embargo invoked by the United States alone. It is a highly industrialized state, better prepared for war than China; and it also is in a better position than China to draw on distant European sources for necessary supplies of war materials.

Third, suppose a war in Europe not involving Great Britain or any other major sea power. The peace of the United States would not be threatened in such a war, regardless of whether or not the American Government permitted trade with the belligerents to continue. If the belligerents were cut off from American exports, the neutral industrial and producing states of Europe would benefit at the expense of our industry and commerce, without our receiving any return for our sacrifice.

Fourth, imagine a war in Europe involving Great Britain but not the rest of the Empire. British sea power would obviously be a factor of which American policy would have to take account if we wished to avoid dangerous complications. If such a war occurred, and if an American embargo were applied to both sides, Canada would take our place as the direct or indirect supplier of British needs—unless, of course, we endeavored also to ration our trade with Canada so as to prevent the shipment of our goods via Canada to Great Britain.

Fifth, take a war in Europe in which the British Empire as a whole participated. This would to all intents and purposes be a world war. The mandatory embargo would of course entail our severing all trade in the embargoed goods with Canada, Australia, South Africa and other British territories. The results of this can be well imagined. There would be fearful suffering alike in our industrial and agricultural areas. Grass would really grow in our streets. A powerful war party would be created. In other words, we would be trying again the experiment of Jefferson, and presumably with the same eventual results.

These are hypothetical situations, and our statement of them may be disputed. What does not seem open to question is that the circumstances in which an automatic embargo would be applied differ radically, that what might be a protective measure in some circumstances would be futile—or worse—in others, that risks might be avoided in one situation by one course and that they would be avoided in another situation by another course, that what might be a legitimate sacrifice to ask of our farmers and factory workers in one case would be considered entirely unwarranted in another.

Obviously there is confusion as to what a trade embargo is expected to accomplish.

Are we trying to keep out of war? Then the logical course would be to apply the embargo only in situations where a continuance of trade is likely to get us into war. This would eliminate an embargo policy in practically every case where none of the belligerents had substantial control of the sea. In those cases our trade could safely continue, and such isolated instances of interference as might occur would be fully covered by adopting a policy of "trade at the trader's risk."

Or are we trying to prevent war? If the purpose of a trade embargo is to prevent the outbreak of war, or the spread of wars that have already begun, then the embargo should be imposed as the result of concerted action by the United States and those other world powers which are important producers and manufacturers of the "sinews of war."

Can we really presume to determine in 1936 what will be the wise policy to follow in *any and every* international situation which may confront the United States in, say, 1940? To attempt it would be to make, in advance and in the dark, momentous political decisions which might have the effect of changing the map of Europe or of Asia.

Let us not forget that in two parts of the world today forces are in motion which potentially are far more dangerous, so far as the maintenance of American peace goes, than an Italian war in Africa. Those who advocate permanent and mandatory legislation which would obligate the President when hostilities are in progress anywhere to stop the export of all materials susceptible of being useful in military operations, should consider what would be the result of applying it in a conflict where Japan or Germany was a party and the United States was neutral. In the one case, the embargo would aid the extension of Japanese domination on the mainland of Asia; cut off from foreign markets, China would be even more helpless to defend herself than she is today. In the other case, it would prevent the democracies of Europe from drawing on the American reservoir of food and other ordinary articles of commerce to check the possible aggression of a rearmed and imperialistic Germany determined to secure the hegemony of the Continent. We need not discuss how likely it is that either Germany or Japan will go to war, or whether either would, if a belligerent, be a menace to us; nor need we attempt to determine in advance how far in a war involving those nations we could with safety to our neutrality permit trade to continue even at the trader's own risk. We need only state that the possibility of conflicts of this nature cannot be excluded, and that it does not seem wise for us to decide today the precise attitude which we would take, in either situation, as regards the shipment from the United States of materials useful in war.

An embargo may suit our interests in the case of war between Italy and Ethiopia. It might prove disastrous to ourselves, and fatal to the principles which we would like to see controlling in international relations, if Congress placed the Government in the position of automatically applying it where the beneficiaries would be countries that proclaim policies which, to put it mildly, cause us uneasiness, and the success of which might weight the world against the kind of government to which the United States is dedicated.

Objections to so double-edged a weapon as the automatic trade embargo might be multiplied. There are, however, arguments in favor of giving the President discretionary power to impose embargoes on certain of the materials useful in war, or possibly all of them, under limitations to be set by Congress as to the purposes to be served and the general circumstances in which the power could be invoked.

We see two situations in which an embargo might play a useful role:

1. Where the conduct of the belligerents on the seas or in the air (for the next war is likely to see airplane attacks on merchant ships) becomes or threatens to become so outrageous that the policy of "trade at the trader's risk" does not seem adequate to prevent our people from demanding redress and urging retaliatory action.

2. Where the coöperation of all the other important neutral states meant that an embargo could be made really effective, hence where it would shorten a war or keep it from spreading, and in this way lessen the risk of our eventually becoming involved.

In the first case, in order to be really effective, the embargo probably would have to cover all the important items in our trade, or at least those which either of the belligerents considered as contraband of war, even including cotton and foodstuffs.

In the second case—that is, where the embargo is adopted as a means to shorten wars—it would only be necessary to deal with the articles which other important producing states also agree to embargo. A coöperative embargo on the export of oil, in a war where the participants were themselves not oil producers, would probably be sufficient to put an end to hostilities.

If the trade embargo is to be imposed only in these two circumstances there obviously must be someone with discretion to determine when the action is justified or necessary. If this power were left with the President it seems likely that he would exercise it cautiously. An embargo would be at best an unpopular move politically and the President would be compelled to satisfy the people that the need to preserve the peace of the United States or to prevent the spread or continuance of war justified the limitation of their normal activities. Further, the enabling legislation of Congress should be drafted so as to limit the power of the President by indicating the specific purposes in view and the general circumstances in which the power could be invoked. Thus Congress would probably stipulate that when invoked the embargo should apply to all belligerents. The limits of the Executive power would be carefully set; and in the event of unforeseen circumstances requiring action, the President would have to go again to Congress to secure appropriate powers.

No attempt should be made to specify in advance the war materials to be covered by any embargo. Obviously a list which omitted articles that either of the belligerents named as contraband would be incomplete. Scientific developments, new discoveries, the changing requirements of warfare, the difficulties of definition—all these make it impossible to draw up any comprehensive list. Congress might, of course, insist on excluding certain articles, for example, foodstuffs and cotton. This would weaken the embargo's usefulness as a protective measure. The chances are that we would more quickly become involved in difficulties if American ships bearing cotton and foodstuffs [3] were sent to the bottom of the sea by belligerents, or if the shipments of these commodities were seized and confiscated, than if ships with cargoes of scrap iron met the same fate.

Americans are apt to resist when their liberty is curtailed. In addition, then, to the requirement that our trade restrictions plainly form an essential part of a definite program for keeping the country out of trouble, they must be as modest as possible. A chance to negotiate before embargoes were imposed might be of assistance in keeping them as painless as possible. A mere threat to close our resources to a belligerent country might be so weighty that in order to avoid the danger the country in question would make concessions as regards our trade with the other belligerent or with neutrals. It will not be easy to steer our policy between Scylla and

---

[3] Both cotton and foodstuffs are likely to be treated as contraband in future wars. So far no progress has been made towards realization of President Hoover's proposal that "all vessels laden solely with food supplies" be placed "on the same footing as hospital ships." (Speech on Armistice Day, 1929. *New York Times*, November 12, 1929.)

Charybdis—between imposing unbearable trade restrictions on our people, and allowing our honor and prestige to become involved in disputes over trade rights in war areas. But that is what we must try to do.

We need not hope that we can remain neutral and at peace and have those who are fighting and suffering love and respect us. At the very best they will be indignant at the mere fact of our neutrality; and if one side feels that the other is able to make more use of our resources, its indignation will increase. This is inevitable, and we must make up our minds to accept the fact. We cannot do more than let the world know that we reserve the right to shut our economic reservoir as and when we find it to be useful in the maintenance of peaceful relations with other nations, and as and when we find that to do so is not intolerably ruinous to our domestic economy. We must say frankly that we shall exercise that right as our own best interest dictates; that if during the progress of a war we have exercised the right, and later decide to reverse our stand because the consequences of the embargo are becoming intolerable, we will do so. We are under no moral or legal obligation to shut off trade with belligerents or to rectify a military advantage accruing to one belligerent through its control of the seas; if we choose to do so it is our own affair; if we reverse that stand it again is our own affair, to be decided by weighing one set of disadvantages against another. The course which we choose should depend upon our own best interest; it should not be influenced by any fetish of neutrality, impartiality or even consistency.

Mr. Walter Lippmann [4] has emphasized the unwisdom and impracticability of changing the rules of our neutrality just before some war breaks out or after it has actually begun. He suggests that we cannot have one neutrality policy to apply to Italy in the Ethiopian war and a different policy if there is a war between Italy and Great Britain or between Germany and the League. Hard cases, he says, make bad law, and he feels that in trying to reconcile our policy with the exigencies of the League's experiment with Mussolini we are in danger of making some very bad American law. Mr. Lippmann is certainly correct in insisting on the importance of drafting our neutrality legislation before war occurs, and in emphasizing that our neutrality statute should be broadly considered and not directed mainly to the very peculiar circumstances of the Italian war in Africa. On the other hand, our neutrality law, we believe, should be sufficiently flexible so that we can forego certain privileges of trade if we think such action is wisest in the particular circumstances, without being too much worried about the precedent which thereby might be created for a different set

[4] *New York Herald Tribune,* December 5 and 7, 1935.

of circumstances when we might decide that it was impracticable or unnecessary to renounce our trade to the same extent. The mere fact that we have decided not to exercise a right in one situation is not necessarily conclusive as to our action in the future. When we pass neutrality legislation we are not primarily interested in making a contribution to international law. Indeed, we do not so much make law as provide a vehicle for making policy—the policy best suited to keeping us out of trouble. Let the legislation be flexible enough, then, to permit us to choose the safest and sanest policy in each crisis as it arises. And let us consciously decide that this is what we are aiming to do, so that the weight of precedent from one crisis will not lie on us too heavily in the next one.

2. *"Trade at Your Own Risk"*

When President Roosevelt on October 5, 1935, stated that American transactions of any character with either Italy or Ethiopia would be at the risk of the trader, he broke definitely with the past. He abandoned the policy of Jefferson and Wilson, and set up a new relationship between the American trader and his government.

Admiral William S. Sims had already joined Mr. Charles Warren, Professor Philip Jessup and others in pointing the way in which the President now moved. Said Admiral Sims:

> *The point of the whole business is this:* We cannot keep out of war and at the same time *enforce the freedom of the seas*—that is, the freedom to make profits out of countries in a death struggle. If a war arises, we must therefore choose between two courses: between great profits with grave risks of war on the one hand; or smaller profits and less risk on the other. . . .
> And the time to decide is now, while we can think calmly and clearly, before war propaganda gets in its deadly work. . . .
> Therefore, let every citizen who has the cause of honorable peace at heart take this stand: *Our trade as a neutral must be at the risk of the traders; our army and navy must not be used to protect this trade. It is a choice of profits or peace. Our country must remain at peace.*[5]

We believe that this policy of what might be called *caveat mercator*—let the trader beware—will probably be as efficacious in preventing the kind of incidents which tend to lead us into war as would much more drastic and elaborate legislation, and without the risks of involvement that more hard-and-fast rules might entail. In particular, it would tend to avoid controversies in case the League decided to lay down a blockade in order to enforce sanctions. Of course it would not eliminate the difficulty of determining the line between legitimate trade with

[5] Radio speech, May 8, 1935, reprinted in pamphlet form by World Peace Foundation.

other neutrals and trade ultimately destined for a belligerent.

We believe that the "trade at your own risk" policy should become a permanent part of American neutrality policy. No legislation by Congress is required. To adopt such a policy lies clearly within the province of the Executive, which is authorized to conduct American foreign relations. It would be a logical continuation, in the Executive field, of the legislation which Congress in its own proper field of action adopted in August 1935. Nevertheless, if Congress by a bipartisan vote should express approval of this policy, the action would tend to establish it as a national policy rather than as an expedient applied to a particular situation by one Administration.

Had we adopted a policy of "trade at your own risk" in 1914 the events of the ensuing years would probably have been very different. Most of our initial troubles with Britain would have been avoided. Germany's complaint that we had bowed to the British blockade and forced her to abandon her own blockade would have been silenced. On the other hand, the sinking of American vessels and the loss of American lives which would have occurred despite the Executive warning would inevitably have tended to arouse American opinion. And what if Germany had sent her submarines across the Atlantic and sunk our ships at our very doors? It is useless to speculate whether this policy would have kept us out of war. All that can be said is that it merits a thorough trial in any future crisis.

Obviously we must protect ourselves against the possibility that the policy of *caveat mercator* might be seized on by our commercial rivals to sweep our trade from the seas and put their own in its stead. We remember that during the World War it was sometimes suggested by our harassed traders that on occasion the British blockade was used for such a purpose. The doctrine therefore cannot be blindly followed. The Executive must be left in a position to see to it that no improper advantage is taken of our traders because of the belief that they are in no event to have the support of their Government in case they get into trouble. The policy must and should mean that interference with American trade may be tolerated only if the interference is incident to the actual conduct of hostilities; it cannot be allowed to mean that we would remain quiescent if the interference had ulterior motives.

3. *Moral Suasion*

We now turn to a further step taken by President Roosevelt and Secretary Hull, the attempt to influence American traders voluntarily to refrain from trade with belligerents in situations where the potential risk involved would not be deterrent enough.

We recall Secretary Hull's statement of November 15, 1935:

> The American people are entitled to know that there are certain commodities such as oil, copper, trucks, tractors, scrap iron, and scrap steel which are essential war materials, although not actually "arms, ammunition, or implements of war," and that according to recent government trade reports a considerably increased amount of these is being exported for war purposes. This class of trade is directly contrary to the policy of this Government as announced in official statements of the President and Secretary of State, as it is also contrary to the general spirit of the recent neutrality act.

We have already discussed the possibility that this policy was adopted, in part at any rate, with a view to preventing any clash between the United States and the states belonging to the League, then engaged in elaborating a system of sanctions for use against Italy. It would seem that if our trade is to be restricted it should be by law and not under moral pressure. Such pressure influences the honest and high-minded trader, and tends to throw the business which he may renounce into the hands of his less scrupulous competitor. Further, we can imagine cases which moral arguments would not touch. For example, they would have no influence whatever upon the agents of belligerents, who either directly or through corporations organized for the purpose might continue to export articles, while American citizens, bowing to the wishes of the Executive, might refrain. Mr. Walter Millis states [6] that during the World War the Germans organized the Bridgeport Projectile Company merely in order to take munitions orders for the Allies, which the company then failed to carry out, thus preëmpting some of the available machinery.

Exercising moral suasion on American exporters is very different from saying to them that their trade is to be at their own risk. The latter policy involves the exercise of an Executive power well within the proper scope of Executive action. The President can at all times determine whether it is useful and necessary to extend or to withhold protection from our citizens; and he can warn them in advance that in certain situations he would withhold it. The fact seems to be that when the Government attempts by moral suasion to restrict American foreign trade, the Executive is attempting to graft a new idea on to our domestic law, and to stop the exercise by American citizens within American territory of activities which are legally open to them. We believe that it is not wise or necessary to do this.

There may be certain limited spheres of activity within which the Government, through the control which it exercises over government-subsidized agencies, particularly shipping, might be able to in-

[6] "Road to War: America, 1914-1917," p. 148.

fluence trade with belligerents without further legislation. There might be further instances—for example in the case of oil—where the Administration might be able to bring about voluntary agreement among those in control of the industry to take concerted action in harmony with governmental wishes. Thus control of most of the available tankers lies in a rather small number of hands; the oil companies might be induced to reach a voluntary agreement to withhold the use of any of their tankers from a particular trade which the Administration felt was contrary to its policy and likely to jeopardize the national safety and welfare.

But this is a difficult and dangerous field of action, and if Congress refuses to give the Executive the legislative authority necessary to deal with war-time trade as seems wisest and safest, we think it would be preferable to abandon entirely the idea of exerting moral pressure and adopt the policy of "trade at the trader's risk."

4. *Quotas*

It has been proposed that, in view of the disadvantages of adopting a total embargo on specific key war materials, and as a more satisfactory and efficient method than moral suasion, an attempt might be made to limit our exports to belligerents to the average peace-time trade. In other words, we would try to distinguish between the normal trade and the abnormal "war profiteering" trade.

This sounds excellent in theory; but in practice we fear that it would be almost impossible of application. To be effective, a quota system would require a strict regimentation and rationing of our exports between clamoring groups of exporters. It would be necessary not only to fix quotas for belligerents, but also for all countries in the general war area and all countries that might serve as transshipment centers. For example, in case we tried to ration shipments to Great Britain, we should probably find other countries—Canada and Mexico, for example—increasing their purchases and sending the goods on to Great Britain, with no result except to increase the cost to the purchaser and to hand over the carrying trade to the vessels of other nations. It is true that during the World War we rationed our shipments to Germany's neutral neighbors; we also rationed all our most important exports to *all* countries and restricted imports from nearly all countries; but this was possible only through the use of a most elaborate wartime machinery, when the United States and the Allies were in complete control of the seas, and when if the neutrals had evidenced a lack of coöperation we should merely have starved them back to a reasonable frame of mind. It would be a highly difficult and complicated undertaking to apply a quota system unless the United States was itself at war and willing to submit to a painful degree of regimentation—and then only in coöperation with other great maritime powers.

5. *"Cash and Carry"*

In view of the difficulties attending the embargo, it has been urged that we continue to sell our goods to belligerents, but say that they must come and get them and carry them home at their own risk in their own ships. Some have spoken of this as the "cash and carry" policy. In an article in *Today,* November 2, 1935, Mr. Bernard M. Baruch calls it the "come and get it" policy. He writes:

> A course which suggests itself as wholly practical is the "come and get it" policy. Under such a policy all shipment of goods by Americans to belligerents would be embargoed, but we should be free to sell goods to any buyer who would send ships to our ports, or charter our ships, and take the goods away wholly at his own risk. We cannot become embroiled if we do that, in disputes over seizures and search, in rows over what is contraband and what is not. We cannot become indignant over losses, because the losses are not ours.

Now, this is not neutrality—not by twenty sea miles. It amounts to giving active assistance to whatever nation has command of the seas. I do not see what we can do about this, or why we should try to do anything about it, so long as our objective is to keep out of war. The only thing we could do about it would be to challenge the command of the seas, and that, of course, is war.

The course of action suggested is passive, not

active, and hence eliminates many grounds for protest by foreign nations. It would not involve anything like as great a loss to American business and agriculture as would a complete embargo, and from this point of view would not seem so likely to break down in practice. Of course the shipments would presumably be financed largely in the United States, and if the goods were lost the burden might fall either upon those who had done the financing or on the insurance companies. They would object, but their objections would not be so likely to rouse the country as would the spectacle of American ships and American goods being sent together to the bottom of the sea. Also, American shipping interests would suffer badly, complain loudly, and demand compensation. But the chief objection to the system would be the colossal difficulty of administering it, especially since the Government would be forced to "ration" shipments to neutral countries so that only those having a bona fide neutral destination could claim the benefit of American ownership. Presumably the method adopted would be to empower the President to forbid American ships to clear for a war area (*i.e.* for a port of a belligerent, or for a neutral port when carrying goods seemingly destined for transshipment to a belligerent), and to prevent the loading on foreign ships of American goods destined for the use of a belligerent unless the foreign ownership of such goods had been established.

CHAPTER IX

CONCLUSION

1. *Avoiding War*

IN THE last two chapters it has been suggested that limitations be placed upon the activities of our citizens when a war is in progress abroad.

We favor restricting American travel on the ships of belligerents, and on any ships entering a war zone. We also favor authorizing an embargo on arms shipments to belligerents, but believe that there are some disadvantages to couching this provision in mandatory terms. Belligerents should be prohibited from floating public loans in this country; there seems no reason why other financial transactions should not be allowed to continue, on the assumption that they would merely take care of such commercial relations as are not prohibited.

The President should have discretionary power, within limits to be set by Congress, to impose embargoes on shipments to belligerents of goods and commodities useful in war; but to instruct him to enforce this provision automatically is dangerous. In order to discourage these shipments to belligerents, and to lessen the danger that our trade will involve our government in disputes, we favor the proclamation of a policy of "trade at your own risk" as being as broad a policy as can safely be adopted in advance for general application in unknown future contingencies. It would be preferable to have the "trade at your own risk" policy stated in advance than for an Administration to attempt on its own responsibility to discourage shipments to belligerents by using what has been called "moral suasion." The "cash and carry" policy would be a much more sweeping application of the same theory which prompts the "trade at your own risk" policy; it would be extremely difficult to administer.

In our consideration of embargoes we have supported the view that the Executive should have the discretion to determine the time when they should be imposed and the articles they should cover. We have not proposed discrimination as between belligerents. Nevertheless, we do not consider the Briand-Kellogg Pact dead nor do we think the country does. We therefore suggest that new neutrality legislation should recognize the possibility of a special procedure if we considered that one of the belligerents had gone to war in violation of its treaty obligations towards the United States, *i.e.* in disregard of its obligations under the Briand-Kellogg Pact not to resort to war as an instrument of national policy.

In such a case the President would present his findings and recommendations to Congress. Then, if Congress concurred, any embargo measure imposed on the state which was defending itself against an attack launched in violation of the Briand-Kellogg Pact would be raised; or alternatively, if an embargo had not been imposed, the embargo would be made effective only against the law-breaking state. The President, of course, already has authority to make such recommendations to Congress; but there seem to be advantages in laying down the broad lines along which our neutrality policy may be developed. The President's initiative in seeking this special authorization would presumably be taken only after consultation with other states, notably the great maritime powers; otherwise the resulting action would probably be ineffective. To those who see some risks in this course we point out that there is at least something to be said for being on the side of the "heaviest guns."

In general, our suggestion is that where the President is given discretionary powers he should have the right to restrict the activities of American citizens in time of war, not to increase them. There seems little risk that he would use such powers arbitrarily or casually, since the restriction of trade would be unpopular and he would have to justify his action by persuading the American people that the temporary losses and inconveniences imposed upon them were more than counterbalanced by the aid given the primary objective of keeping out of war.

A sweeping and mandatory embargo on all commodities and goods would produce monstrous results in most of the wars which are conceivable and in which the United States would hope to be neutral. It would penalize our trade unnecessarily and probably would end by producing such a revulsion of feeling that we would abandon even reasonable restrictions on our activities and revert to the dangerous policies which in Jefferson's day brought us into war and which a century later led us into the World War.

2. *Maintaining Peace*

Our purpose in this small book has been to set forth the pros and cons of the various methods suggested in Congress and the press for the United States to escape being entangled in war. It is advisable to adopt some of them. Some of them may prove useful. But it should be understood that they are mere palliatives. The only sure way for the United States to escape entanglement in foreign wars is for there to be no wars. We can stay out of wars between minor states; but minor wars easily become major wars; and we have no assurance that any expedients we may adopt to insulate ourselves against wars between great powers will really work.

For this reason it seems impossible to believe that the elaboration of a complicated system of safeguards designed to protect American neutrality can be the sole or even the principal aim of American foreign policy. The Government, both in its executive and legislative branches, must take constant account of the fact that the United States has a continuing responsibility which is broader than the aim to escape from some particular difficulty or danger. The United States has an interest that hostilities do not occur anywhere, an interest to bring them to as prompt an end as possible when they do occur, and a responsibility to help prevent them from occurring.

We speak of American responsibility with diffidence; the word has been over-worked and is unpopular. But the responsibility is there. We have a moral responsibility to help and not to hinder world peace because we are a great nation, magnificently endowed with natural resources, almost a continent in ourselves, fortunately situated between two oceans, and priding ourselves on possessing a broad educational system which makes our citizens progressive and open-minded. In conformity with the civilized principle that power confers responsibility, we have the duty to support any reasonable move to organize the world more effectively for peace.

The United States also has a direct, material, selfish interest that hostilities shall not break out anywhere. War is a hungry octopus. Combatants need supplies from every land. They buy, which in itself is dangerous enough because it enlists the sympathies of those from whom they purchase; when they become desperate they ravage the seas, seizing what they need or what their enemy needs; and they can sink enemy and neutral vessels alike "without trace." It is hard enough in any event to keep our feelings under control. It has become harder since science has arranged to bring the arguments of both sides under our eyes almost before the events on which they are based have occurred, and to din them into our ears through radio accounts from eye witnesses on the field of battle. It is hard, too, to restrain our natural desire for work and profit. Our farmers and miners and cotton pickers and steel workers and automobile builders all produce things which a combatant wants and will buy if he can; for us to sell or not to sell becomes a choice between unusual profit and unusual loss, not for great captains of industry and bankers only but for the machine worker, the clerk and the farm hand.

In this view, the duty to help prevent wars is not primarily one which the United States owes to other nations. It is a duty which we owe to ourselves and which our Government owes to its people. Self-interest should determine our course of action. Let it be enlightened self-interest. Sections of our press and many of our political leaders preach to us that collaboration for peace is dangerous, that it would embroil us in European and Asiatic affairs of no concern to us. "Internationalism," "foreign entanglements," "back-door entrance to the League," and other catch phrases are used to try to drive us into an isolation which would deprive us of influence in world councils where the issue is peace or war. That we should reserve independence of judgment and refuse to commit ourselves in advance regarding our course of action in individual situations is only prudent. But if those controlling the course of American foreign policy, whether in the executive or legislative branch, place the United States in a position where it could not use its influence on specific occasions to turn the balance in favor of peace, then they are the ones who would be taking the grave responsibility of exposing this country again to the dangers of war—not merely to the inconveniences caused by the fact that other peoples are at war, and not just to the common economic losses caused the whole world by any major modern war—but the risk of eventually being driven into war ourselves.

There is much that we can do to bring the policy which we would follow as a neutral into line with our real national interests. But no neutrality legislation can give us the advantages of an isolation which does not in fact exist. We are not a planet by ourselves, but only a continent between two oceans no longer so wide as they were when in the past we fought on them in defense of our asserted rights of trade and the lives of our citizens.

APPENDICES

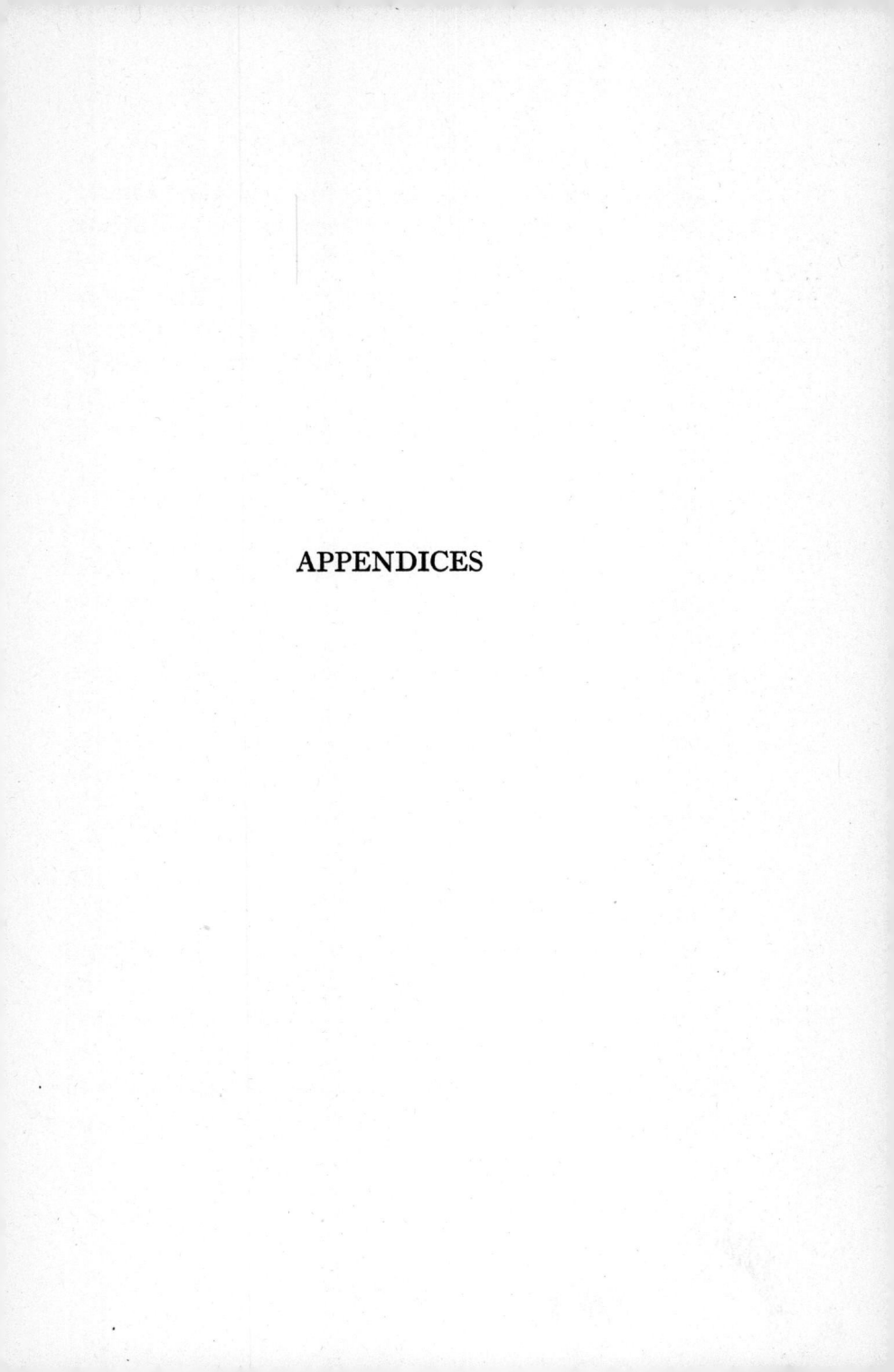

APPENDIX 1

PRESIDENT WILSON'S PROCLAMATION OF NEUTRALITY, AUGUST 4, 1914 [1]

Whereas a state of war unhappily exists between Austria-Hungary and Serbia and between Germany and Russia and between Germany and France; [2] and whereas the United States is on terms of friendship and amity with the contending powers, and with the persons inhabiting their several dominions;

And Whereas there are citizens of the United States residing within the territories or dominions of each of the said belligerents, and carrying on commerce, trade, or other business or pursuits therein;

And Whereas there are subjects of each of the said belligerents residing within the territory or jurisdiction of the United States, and carrying on commerce, trade, or other business or pursuits therein;

And Whereas the laws and treaties of the United States, without interfering with the free expression of opinion and sympathy, or with the commercial manufacture or sale of arms or munitions of war, nevertheless impose upon all persons who may be within their territory and jurisdiction the duty of an impartial neutrality during the existence of the contest;

And Whereas it is the duty of a neutral government not to permit or suffer the making of its waters subservient to the purposes of war;

Now, therefore, I, Woodrow Wilson, President of the United States of America, in order to preserve the neutrality

[1] "Papers Relating to the Foreign Relations of the United States," 1914, Supplement, The World War, p. 547-51.
[2] Additional proclamations identical in character were subsequently issued for the war between Germany and Great Britain, Austria-Hungary and Russia, etc., etc.

of the United States and of its citizens and of persons within its territory and jurisdiction, and to enforce its laws and treaties, and in order that all persons, being warned of the general tenor of the laws and treaties of the United States in this behalf, and of the law of nations, may thus be prevented from any violation of the same, do hereby declare and proclaim that by certain provisions of the act approved on the 4th day of March, A. D. 1909, commonly known as the "Penal Code of the United States," the following acts are forbidden to be done, under severe penalties, within the territory and jurisdiction of the United States, to wit:

1. Accepting and exercising a commission to serve either of the said belligerents by land or by sea against the other belligerent.

2. Enlisting or entering into the service of either of said belligerents as a soldier, or as a marine, or seaman on board of any vessel of war, letter of marque, or privateer.

3. Hiring or retaining another person to enlist or enter himself in the service of either of the said belligerents as a soldier, or as a marine, or seaman on board of any vessel of war, letter of marque, or privateer.

4. Hiring another person to go beyond the limits or jurisdiction of the United States with intent to be enlisted as aforesaid.

5. Hiring another person to go beyond the limits of the United States with intent to be entered into service as aforesaid.

6. Retaining another person to go beyond the limits of the United States with intent to be enlisted as aforesaid.

7. Retaining another person to go beyond the limits of the United States with intent to be entered into service as aforesaid. (But the said act is not to be construed to extend to a citizen or subject of either belligerent who, being tran-

siently within the United States, shall, on board of any vessel of war, which, at the time of its arrival within the United States, was fitted and equipped as such vessel of war, enlist or enter himself or hire or retain another subject or citizen of the same belligerent, who is transiently within the United States, to enlist or enter himself to serve such belligerent on board such vessel of war, if the United States shall then be at peace with such belligerent.)

8. Fitting out and arming, or attempting to fit out and arm, or procuring to be fitted out and armed, or knowingly being concerned in the furnishing, fitting out, or arming of any ship or vessel with intent that such ship or vessel shall be employed in the service of either of the said belligerents.

9. Issuing or delivering a commission within the territory or jurisdiction of the United States for any ship or vessel to the intent that she may be employed as aforesaid.

10. Increasing or augmenting, or procuring to be increased or augmented, or knowingly being concerned in increasing or augmenting, the force of any ship of war, cruiser, or other armed vessel, which at the time of her arrival within the United States was a ship of war, cruiser, or armed vessel in the service of either of the said belligerents, or belonging to the subjects of either, by adding to the number of guns of such vessels, or by changing those on board of her for guns of a larger caliber, or by the addition thereto of any equipment solely applicable to war.

11. Beginning or setting on foot or providing or preparing the means for any military expedition or enterprise to be carried on from the territory or jurisdiction of the United States against the territories or dominions of either of the said belligerents.

And I do hereby further declare and proclaim that any frequenting and use of the waters within the territorial jurisdiction of the United States by the armed vessels of a belligerent, whether public ships or privateers, for the purpose of preparing for hostile operations, or as posts of observation upon the ships of war or privateers or merchant vessels of a belligerent lying within or being about to enter the jurisdiction of the United States, must be regarded as unfriendly and offensive, and in violation of that neutrality which it is the determination of this government to observe; and to the end that the hazard and inconvenience of such apprehended practices may be avoided, I further proclaim and declare that from and after the fifth day of August instant, and during the continuance of the present hostilities between Austria-Hungary and Serbia, and Germany and Russia and Germany and France, no ship of war or privateer of any belligerent shall be permitted to make use of any port, harbor, roadstead, or other waters within the jurisdiction of the United States as a station or place of resort for any warlike purpose or for the purpose of obtaining any facilities of warlike equipment; and no ship of war or privateer of either belligerent shall be permitted to sail out of or leave any port, harbor, roadstead, or waters subject to the jurisdiction of the United States from which a vessel of an opposing belligerent (whether the same shall be a ship of war, a privateer, or a merchant ship) shall have previously departed, until after the expiration of at least twenty-four hours from the departure of such last-mentioned vessel beyond the jurisdiction of the United States.

If any ship of war or privateer of a belligerent shall, after the time this notification takes place, enter any port, harbor, roadstead, or waters of the United States, such vessel shall be required to depart and to put to sea within twenty-four hours after her entrance into such port, harbor, roadstead, or waters, except in case of stress of weather or of her requiring provisions or things necessary for the subsistence of her crew, or for repairs; in any of which cases the authorities of the port, or of the nearest port (as the case may be), shall require her to put to sea as soon as possible after the expiration of such period of twenty-four hours, without permitting her to take in supplies beyond what may be necessary for her immediate use; and no such vessel which may have been permitted to remain within the waters of the United States for the purpose of repair shall continue within such port, harbor, roadstead, or waters for a longer period than twenty-four hours after her necessary repairs shall have been completed, unless within such twenty-four hours a vessel, whether ship of war, privateer, or merchant ship of an opposing belligerent, shall have departed therefrom, in which case the time limited for the departure of such ship of war or privateer shall be extended so far as may be necessary to secure an interval of not less than twenty-four hours between such departure and that of any ship of war, privateer, or merchant ship of an opposing belligerent which may have previously quit the same port, harbor, roadstead, or waters.

No ship of war or privateer of a belligerent shall be detained in any port, harbor, roadstead, or waters of the United States more than twenty-four hours, by reason of the successive departures from such port, harbor, roadstead, or waters of more than one vessel of an opposing belligerent. But if there be several vessels of opposing belligerents in the same port, harbor, roadstead, or waters, the order of their departure therefrom shall be so arranged so as to afford the opportunity of leaving alternately to the vessels of the opposing belligerents, and to cause the least detention consistent with the objects of this proclamation.

No ship of war or privateer of a belligerent shall be permitted, while in any port, harbor, roadstead, or waters within the jurisdiction of the United States, to take in any supplies except provisions and such other things as may be requisite for the subsistence of her crew, and except so much coal only as may be sufficient to carry such vessel, if without any sail power, to the nearest port of her own country; or in case the vessel is rigged to go under sail, and may also be propelled by steam power, then with half the quantity of coal which she would be entitled to receive, if dependent upon steam alone, and no coal shall be again supplied to any such ship of war or privateer in the same or any other port, harbor, roadstead, or waters of the United States, without special permission, until after the expiration of three months from the time when such coal may have been last supplied to her within the waters of the United States, unless such ship of war or privateer shall, since last thus supplied, have entered a port of the government to which she belongs.

And I do further declare and proclaim that the statutes and the treaties of the United States and the law of nations alike require that no person, within the territory and jurisdiction of the United States, shall take part, directly or indirectly, in the said wars, but shall remain at peace with all of the said belligerents, and shall maintain a strict and impartial neutrality.

And I do hereby enjoin all citizens of the United States, and all persons residing or being within the territory or jurisdiction of the United States, to observe the laws thereof, and to commit no act contrary to the provisions of the said statutes or treaties or in violation of the law of nations in that behalf.

And I do hereby warn all citizens of the United States, and all persons residing or being within its territory or jurisdiction that, while the free and full expression of sympathies in public and private is not restricted by the laws of the United States, military forces in aid of a belligerent can not lawfully be originated or organized within its jurisdiction; and that, while all persons may lawfully and without restriction by reason of the aforesaid state of war manufacture and sell within the United States arms and munitions of war, and other articles ordinarily known as "contraband of war," yet they can not carry such articles upon the high seas for the use or service of a belligerent, nor can they transport soldiers and officers of a belligerent, or attempt to break any blockade which may be lawfully established and maintained during the said war without incurring the risk of hostile capture and the penalties denounced by the law of nations in that behalf.

And I do hereby give notice that all citizens of the United States and others who may claim the protection of this government, who may misconduct themselves in the premises, will do so at their peril, and that they can in no wise obtain any protection from the government of the United States against the consequences of their misconduct.

In witness whereof I have hereunto set my hand and caused the seal of the United States to be affixed.

Done at the City of Washington this fourth day of August in the year of our Lord one thousand nine hundred and fourteen and of the Independence of the United States of America the one hundred and thirty-ninth.

WOODROW WILSON.

By the President:

WILLIAM JENNINGS BRYAN,
    Secretary of State.

APPENDIX 2

PRESIDENT WILSON'S STATEMENT OF AUGUST 19, 1914 [1]

My Fellow Countrymen: I suppose that every thoughtful man in America has asked himself, during these last troubled weeks, what influence the European war may exert upon the United States, and I take the liberty of addressing a few words to you in order to point out that it is entirely within our own choice what its effects upon us will be and to urge very earnestly upon you the sort of speech and conduct which will best safeguard the Nation against distress and disaster.

The effect of the war upon the United States will depend upon what American citizens say and do. Every man who really loves America will act and speak in the true spirit of neutrality, which is the spirit of impartiality and fairness and friendliness to all concerned. The spirit of the nation in this critical matter will be determined largely by what individuals and society and those gathered in public meetings do and say, upon what newspapers and magazines contain, upon what ministers utter in their pulpits, and men proclaim as their opinions on the street.

The people of the United States are drawn from many nations, and chiefly from the nations now at war. It is natural and inevitable that there should be the utmost variety of sympathy and desire among them with regard to the issues and circumstances of the conflict. Some will wish one nation, others another, to succeed in the momentous struggle. It will be easy to excite passion and difficult to allay it. Those responsible for exciting it will assume a heavy responsibility, responsibility for no less a thing than that the people of the United States, whose love of their country and whose loyalty to its Government should unite them as Amer-

---

[1] "Papers Relating to the Foreign Relations of the United States," 1914, Supplement, The World War, p. 551-2.

icans all, bound in honor and affection to think first of her and her interests, may be divided in camps of hostile opinion, hot against each other, involved in the war itself in impulse and opinion if not in action.

Such divisions among us would be fatal to our peace of mind and might seriously stand in the way of the proper performance of our duty as the one great nation at peace, the one people holding itself ready to play a part of impartial mediation and speak the counsels of peace and accommodation, not as a partisan, but as a friend.

I venture, therefore, my fellow countrymen, to speak a solemn word of warning to you against that deepest, most subtle, most essential breach of neutrality which may spring out of partisanship, out of passionately taking sides. The United States must be neutral in fact as well as in name during these days that are to try men's souls. We must be impartial in thought as well as in action, must put a curb upon our sentiments as well as upon every transaction that might be construed as a preference of one party to the struggle before another.

My thought is of America. I am speaking, I feel sure, the earnest wish and purpose of every thoughtful American that this great country of ours, which is, of course, the first in our thoughts and in our hearts, should show herself in this time of peculiar trial a nation fit beyond others to exhibit the fine poise of undisturbed judgment, the dignity of self-control, the efficiency of dispassionate action; a nation that neither sits in judgment upon others nor is disturbed in her own counsels and which keeps herself fit and free to do what is honest and disinterested and truly serviceable for the peace of the world.

Shall we not resolve to put upon ourselves the restraints which will bring to our people the happiness and the great and lasting influence for peace we covet for them?

WOODROW WILSON.

APPENDIX 3

THE ACT OF APRIL 13, 1934 [1]
(The So-Called "Johnson Act")

An Act to prohibit financial transactions with any foreign government in default on its obligations to the United States.

Be it enacted by the Senate and House of Representatives of the United States of America in Congress assembled, That hereafter it shall be unlawful within the United States or any place subject to the jurisdiction of the United States for any person to purchase or sell the bonds, securities, or other obligations of, any foreign government or political subdivision thereof or any organization or association acting for or on behalf of a foreign government or political subdivision thereof, issued after the passage of this Act, or to make any loan to such foreign government, political subdivision, organization, or association, except a renewal or adjustment of existing indebtedness while such government, political subdivision, organization, or association, is in default in the payment of its obligations, or any part thereof, to the Government of the United States. Any person violating the provisions of this Act shall upon conviction thereof be fined not more than $10,000 or imprisoned for not more than five years, or both.

SEC. 2. As used in this Act the term "person" includes individual, partnership, corporation, or association other than a public corporation created by or pursuant to special authorization of Congress, or a corporation in which the Government of the United States has or exercises a controlling interest through stock ownership or otherwise.

Approved, April 13, 1934.

[1] Public, No. 151, 73d Congress [S. 682].

APPENDIX 4

UNITED STATES NEUTRALITY LAWS, AS REVISED TO JANUARY 3, 1935 [1]

CHAPTER 2.—OFFENSES AGAINST NEUTRALITY

Criminal Code, section 9

SECTION 21. *Accepting commission to serve against friendly power.* Every citizen of the United States who, within the territory or jurisdiction thereof, accepts and exercises a commission to serve a foreign prince, state, colony, district, or people, in war, by land or by sea, against any prince, state, colony, district, or people, with whom the United States are at peace, shall be fined not more than $2,000 and imprisoned not more than three years. (R. S. § 5281; Mar. 4, 1909, c. 321, § 9, 35 Stat. 1089.)

Criminal Code, section 10, amended

§ 22. *Enlisting in foreign service; exceptions.* Whoever, within the territory or jurisdiction of the United States, enlists or enters himself, or hires or retains another person to enlist or enter himself, or to go beyond the limits or jurisdiction of the United States with intent to be enlisted or entered in the service of any foreign prince, state, colony, district, or people as a soldier or as a marine or seaman on board of any vessel of war, letter of marque, or privateer shall be fined not more than $1,000 and imprisoned not more than three years: *Provided,* That this section shall not apply to citizens or subjects of any country engaged in war with a country with which the United States is at war, unless such citizen or subject of such foreign country shall hire or solicit a citizen of the United States to enlist or go beyond the jurisdiction of the United States with intent to enlist or enter the

[1] Chapter 2 of Title 18 of the Code of the Laws of the United States of America of a general and permanent character in force January 3, 1935.

service of a foreign country. Enlistments under this proviso shall be under regulations prescribed by the Secretary of War. (R. S. § 5282; Mar. 4, 1909, c. 321, § 10, 35 Stat. 1089; May 7, 1917, c. 11, 40 Stat. 39.)

Criminal Code, section 11

§ 23. *Arming vessels against friendly powers; forfeiture of vessel.* Whoever, within the territory or jurisdiction of the United States, fits out and arms, or attempts to fit out and arm, or procures to be fitted out and armed, or knowingly is concerned in the furnishing, fitting out, or arming of any vessel, with intent that such vessel shall be employed in the service of any foreign prince, or state, or of any colony, district, or people, to cruise, or commit hostilities against the subjects, citizens, or property of any foreign prince or state, or of any colony, district, or people, with whom the United States are at peace, or whoever issues or delivers a commission within the territory or jurisdiction of the United States for any vessel, to the intent that she may be so employed, shall be fined not more than $10,000 and imprisoned not more than three years. And every such vessel, her tackle, apparel, and furniture, together with all materials, arms, ammunition, and stores which may have been procured for the building and equipment thereof, shall be forfeited; one half to the use of the informer and the other half to the use of the United States. (R. S. § 5283; Mar. 4, 1909, c. 321, § 11, 35 Stat. 1090.)

Criminal Code, section 12

§ 24. *Augmenting force of foreign armed vessel.* Whoever, within the territory or jurisdiction of the United States, increases or augments, or procures to be increased or augmented, or knowingly is concerned in increasing or augmenting, the force of any ship of war, cruiser, or other armed vessel which, at the time of her arrival within the United States, was a ship of war, or cruiser, or armed vessel, in the service of any foreign prince or state, or of any colony, district, or people, or belonging to the subjects or citizens of any such prince or state, colony, district, or people, the same being at war with any foreign prince or state, or of any colony, district, or people, with whom the United States are at peace, by adding to the number of the guns of such vessel, or by changing those on board of her for guns of a larger caliber, or by adding thereto any equipment solely applicable to war, shall be fined not more than $1,000 and imprisoned not more than one year. (R. S. § 5285; Mar. 4, 1909, c. 321, § 12, 35 Stat. 1090.)

Criminal Code, section 13, amended

§ 25. *Organizing military expedition against friendly power.* Whoever, within the territory or jurisdiction of the United States or of any of its possessions, knowingly begins or sets on foot or provides or prepares a means for or furnishes the money for, or who takes part in, any military or naval expedition or enterprise to be carried on from thence against the territory or dominion of any foreign prince or state, or of any colony, district, or people with whom the United States is at peace, shall be fined not more than $3,000 or imprisoned not more than three years, or both. (R. S. § 5286; Mar. 4, 1909, c. 321, § 13, 35 Stat. 1090; June 15, 1917, c. 30, Title V, § 8, 40 Stat. 223.)

Criminal Code, section 14

§ 26. *Enforcement by courts; employment of land or naval forces.* The district courts shall take cognizance of all complaints, by whomsoever instituted, in cases of captures made within the waters of the United States, or within a marine league of the coasts or shores thereof. In every case in which a vessel is fitted out and armed, or attempted to be fitted out and armed, or in which the force of any vessel of war, cruiser, or other armed vessel is increased or augmented, or in which any military expedition or enterprise is begun or set on foot, contrary to the provisions and prohibitions of this chapter; and in every case of the capture of a vessel within the jurisdiction or protection of the United States as before defined; and in every case in which any process issuing out of any court of the United States is disobeyed or resisted by any person having the custody of any vessel of war, cruiser, or other armed vessel of any foreign prince or state, or of any colony, district, or people, or of any subjects or citizens of any foreign prince or state, or of any colony, district, or people, it shall be lawful for the President or such other person as he shall have empowered for that purpose, to employ such part of the land or naval forces of the United States, or of the militia thereof, for the purpose of taking possession of and detaining any such vessel, with her prizes, if any, in order to enforce the execution of the prohibitions and penalties of this chapter, and the restoring of such prizes in the cases in which restoration shall be adjudged; and also for the purpose of preventing the carrying on of any such expedition or enterprise from the territory or jurisdiction of the United States against the territory or dominion of any foreign prince or state, or of any colony, district, or people with whom the United States are at peace. (R. S. § 5287; Mar. 4, 1909, c. 321, §14, 35 Stat. 1090.)

Criminal Code, section 15, amended

§ 27. *Compelling foreign vessels to depart.* It shall be lawful for the President to employ such part of the land or naval forces of the United States, or of the militia thereof, as he may deem necessary to compel any foreign vessel to depart from the United States or any of its possessions in all cases in which, by the law of nations or the treaties of the United States, it ought not to remain, and to detain or prevent any foreign vessel from so departing in all cases in which, by the law of nations or the treaties of the United States, it is not entitled to depart. (R. S. § 5288; Mar. 4, 1909, c. 321, § 15, 35 Stat. 1091; June 15, 1917, c. 30, Title V, § 10, 40 Stat. 223.)

Criminal Code, section 16

§ 28. *Bonds from armed vessels on clearing.* The owners or consignees of every armed vessel sailing out of the ports of, or under the jurisdiction of, the United States, belonging wholly or in part to citizens thereof, shall, before clearing out the same, give bond to the United States, with sufficient sureties, in double the amount of the value of the vessel and cargo on board, including her armament, conditioned that the vessel shall not be employed by such owners to cruise or commit hostilities against the subjects, citizens, or property of any foreign prince or state, or of any colony, district, or people with whom the United States are at peace. (R. S. § 5289; Mar. 4, 1909, c. 321, § 16, 35 Stat. 1091.)

Criminal Code, section 17

§ 29. *Detention by collectors of customs.* The several collectors of the customs shall detain any vessel manifestly built for warlike purposes, and about to depart the United States, or any place subject to the jurisdiction thereof, the cargo of which principally consists of arms and munitions of war, when the number of men shipped on board, or other circumstances, render it probable that such vessel is intended to be employed by the owners to cruise or commit hostilities upon the subjects, citizens, or property of any foreign prince or state, or of any colony, district, or people with whom the United States are at peace, until the decision of the President is had thereon, or until the owner gives such bond and security as is required of the owners of armed vessels by section 28 of this title. (R. S. § 5290; Mar. 4, 1909, c. 321, § 17, 35 Stat. 1091.)

Criminal Code, section 18

§ 30. *Construction of chapter; transient aliens; prosecutions for treason or piracy.* The provisions of sections 21 to 29 of this title shall not be construed to extend to any subject or citizen of any foreign prince, state, colony, district, or people who is transiently within the United States and enlists or enters himself on board of any vessel of war, letter of marque, or privateer, which at the time of its arrival within the United States was fitted and equipped as such, or hires or retains another subject or citizen of the same foreign prince, state, colony, district, or people who is transiently within the United States to enlist or enter himself to serve such foreign prince, state, colony, district, or people on board such vessel of war, letter of marque, or privateer, if the United States shall then be at peace with such foreign prince, state, colony, district, or people. Nor shall they be construed to prevent the prosecution or punishment of treason, or of any piracy defined by the laws of the United States. (R. S. § 5291; Mar. 4, 1909, c. 321, § 18, 35 Stat. 1091.)

§ 31. *Enforcement of neutrality; withholding clearance papers from vessels.* During a war in which the United States is a neutral nation, the President, or any person thereunto authorized by him, may withhold clearance from or to any vessel, domestic or foreign, which is required by law to secure clearance before departing from port or from the jurisdiction of the United States, or, by service of formal notice upon the owner, master, or person in command or having charge of any domestic vessel not required by law to secure clearances before so departing, to forbid its departure from port or from the jurisdiction of the United States, whenever there is reasonable cause to believe that any such vessel, domestic or foreign, whether requiring clearance or not, is about to carry fuel, arms, ammunition, men, supplies, dispatches, or information to any warship, tender, or supply ship of a foreign belligerent nation in violation of the laws, treaties, or obligations of the United States under the law of nations; and it shall thereupon be unlawful for such vessel to depart. (June 15, 1917, c. 30, Title V, § 1, 40 Stat. 221.)

§ 32. *Same; detention of armed vessels.* During a war in which the United States is a neutral nation, the President, or any person thereunto authorized by him, may detain any armed vessel owned wholly or in part by American citizens, or any vessel, domestic or foreign (other than one which has entered the ports of the United States as a public vessel), which is manifestly built for warlike purposes or has been converted or adapted from a private vessel to one suitable for warlike use, until the owner or master, or person having charge of such vessel, shall furnish proof satisfactory to the President, or to the person duly authorized by him, that the vessel will not be employed by the said owners, or master, or person having charge thereof, to cruise against or commit or attempt to commit hostilities upon the subjects, citizens, or property of any foreign prince or state, or of any colony, district, or people with which the United States is at peace, and that the said vessel will not be sold or delivered to any belligerent nation, or to an agent, officer, or citizen of such nation, by them or any of them, within the jurisdiction of the United States, or, having left that jurisdiction, upon the high seas. (June 15, 1917, c. 30, Title V, § 2, 40 Stat. 221.)

§ 33. *Same; sending out armed vessel with intent to deliver to belligerent nation.* During a war in which the United States is a neutral nation, it shall be unlawful to send out of the jurisdiction of the United States any vessel built, armed, or equipped as a vessel of war, or converted from a private vessel into a vessel of war, with any intent or under any agreement or contract, written or oral, that such vessel shall be delivered to a belligerent nation, or to an agent, officer, or citizen of such nation, or with reasonable cause to believe that the said vessel shall or will be employed in the service of any such belligerent nation after its departure from the jurisdiction of the United States. (June 15, 1917, c. 30, Title V, § 3, 40 Stat. 222.)

§ 34. *Same; statement from master that cargo will not be delivered to other vessels.* During a war in which the United States is a neutral nation, in addition to the facts required by sections 91, 92, and 94 of Title 46 to be set out in the masters' and shippers' manifests before clearance will be issued to vessels bound to foreign ports, each of which sections is hereby declared to be and is continued in full force and effect, every master or person having charge or command of any vessel, domestic or foreign, whether requiring clearance or not, before departure of such vessel from port shall deliver to the collector of customs for the district wherein such vessel is then located a statement, duly verified by oath, that the cargo or any part of the cargo is or is not to be delivered to other vessels in port or to be transshipped on the high seas, and, if it is to be so delivered or transshipped, stating the kind and quantities and the value of the total quantity of each kind of article so to be delivered or transshipped, and the name of the person, corporation, vessel, or government to whom the delivery or transshipment is to be made; and the owners, shippers, or consignors of the cargo of such vessel shall in the same manner and under the same conditions deliver to the collector like statements under oath as to the cargo or the parts thereof laden or shipped by them, respectively. (June 15, 1917, c. 30, Title V, § 4, 40 Stat. 222.)

§ 35. *Same; forbidding departure of vessels.* Whenever it appears that the vessel is not entitled to clearance or whenever there is reasonable cause to believe that the additional statements under oath required in section 34 of this title are false, the collector of customs for the district in which the vessel is located may, subject to review by the Secretary of Commerce, refuse clearance to any vessel, domestic or foreign, and by formal notice served upon the owners, master, or person or persons in command or charge of any domestic vessel for which clearance is not required by law, forbid the departure of the vessel from the port or from the jurisdiction of the United States; and it shall thereupon be unlawful for the vessel to depart. (June 15, 1917, c. 30, Title V, § 5, 40 Stat. 222.)

§ 36. *Same; unlawful taking of vessel out of port.* Whoever, in violation of any of the provisions of sections 25, 27, and 31 to 38 of this title, shall take, or attempt or conspire to take, or authorize the taking of any such vessel, out of port or from the jurisdiction of the United States, shall be fined not more than $10,000 or imprisoned not more than five years, or both; and, in addition, such vessel, her tackle, apparel, furniture, equipment, and her cargo shall be forfeited to the United States. (June 15, 1917, c. 30, Title V, § 6, 40 Stat. 222.)

§ 37. *Same; internment of person belonging to armed land or naval forces of belligerent nation; arrest; punishment for aiding escape.* Whoever, being a person belonging to the armed land or naval forces of a belligerent nation or belligerent faction of any nation and being interned in the United States, in accordance with the law of nations, shall leave or attempt to leave said jurisdiction, or shall leave or attempt to leave the limits of internment in which freedom of movement has been allowed, without permission from the proper official of the United States in charge, or shall willfully overstay a leave of absence granted by such official, shall be subject to arrest by any marshal or deputy marshal of the United States, or by the military or naval authorities thereof, and shall be returned to the place of internment and there confined and safely kept for such period of time as the official of the United States in charge shall direct; and whoever, within the jurisdiction of the United States and subject thereto, shall aid or entice any interned person to escape or attempt to escape from the jurisdiction of the United States, or from the limits of internment prescribed, shall be fined not more than $1,000 or imprisoned not more than one year, or both. (June 15, 1917, c. 30, Title V, § 7, 40 Stat. 223.)

§ 38. *Same; enforcement of sections 25, 27, and 31 to 37 of this title.* The President may employ such part of the land or naval forces of the United States as he may deem necessary to carry out the purposes of sections 25, 27, and

31 to 37 of this title. (June 15, 1917, c. 30, Title V, § 9, 40 Stat. 223.)

§ 39. *Same; United States defined; jurisdiction of offenses; prior offenses; partial invalidity of provisions.* The term "United States," as used in sections 25, 27, and 31 to 38 of this title, includes the Canal Zone, and all territory and waters, continental or insular, subject to the jurisdiction of the United States. The several courts of first instance in the Philippine Islands and the district court of the Canal Zone shall have jurisdiction of offenses under said sections 25, 27, and 31 to 38 committed within their respective districts, and concurrent jurisdiction with the district courts of the United States of offenses thereunder committed upon the high seas, and of conspiracies to commit such offenses, as defined by section 88 of this title, and the provisions of said section 88, for the purposes of sections 25, 27, and 31 to 38 of this title, are extended to the Philippine Islands and to the Canal Zone. Offenses committed and penalties, forfeitures, or liabilities incurred prior to June 15, 1917, under any law embraced in or changed, modified, or repealed by sections 25, 27, and 31 to 38 may be prosecuted and punished, and suits and proceedings for causes arising or acts done or committed prior to June 15, 1917, may be commenced and prosecuted, in the same manner and with the same effect as if said sections 25, 27, and 31 to 38 had not been passed. If any clause, sentence, paragraph, or part of sections 25, 27, and 31 to 38 shall for any reason be adjudged by any court of competent jurisdiction to be invalid, such judgment shall not affect, impair, or invalidate the remainder thereof but shall be confined in its operation to the clause, sentence, paragraph, or part thereof directly involved in the controversy in which such judgment shall have been rendered. (June 15, 1917, c. 30, Title XIII, §§ 1 to 4, 40 Stat. 231.)

APPENDIX 5

THE NEUTRALITY ACT OF AUGUST 31, 1935 [1]

Resolved by the Senate and House of Representatives of the United States of America in Congress assembled, That upon the outbreak or during the progress of war between, or among, two or more foreign states, the President shall proclaim such fact, and it shall thereafter be unlawful to export arms, ammunition, or implements of war from any place in the United States, or possessions of the United States, to any port of such belligerent states, or to any neutral port for transshipment to, or for the use of, a belligerent country.

The President, by proclamation, shall definitely enumerate the arms, ammunition, or implements of war, the export of which is prohibited by this Act.

The President may, from time to time, by proclamation, extend such embargo upon the export of arms, ammunition, or implements of war to other states as and when they may become involved in such war.

Whoever, in violation of any of the provisions of this section, shall export, or attempt to export, or cause to be exported, arms, ammunition, or implements of war from the United States, or any of its possessions, shall be fined not more than $10,000 or imprisoned not more than five years, or both, and the property, vessel, or vehicle containing the same shall be subject to the provisions of sections 1 to 8, inclusive, title 6, chapter 30, of the Act approved June 15, 1917 (40 Stat. 223-225; U. S. C., title 22, secs. 238-245).

In the case of the forfeiture of any arms, ammunition, or implements of war by reason of a violation of this Act, no public or private sale shall be required; but such arms, ammunition, or implements of war shall be delivered to the Secretary of War for such use or disposal thereof as shall be approved by the President of the United States.

[1] Public Resolution, No. 67, 74th Congress [S. J. Res. 173]. See also Addendum 2, p. 179.

When in the judgment of the President the conditions which have caused him to issue his proclamation have ceased to exist he shall revoke the same and the provisions hereof shall thereupon cease to apply.

Except with respect to prosecutions committed or forfeitures incurred prior to March 1, 1936, this section and all proclamations issued thereunder shall not be effective after February 29, 1936.

Sec. 2. That for the purposes of this Act—

(a) The term "Board" means the National Munitions Control Board which is hereby established to carry out the provisions of this Act. The Board shall consist of the Secretary of State, who shall be chairman and executive officer of the Board; the Secretary of the Treasury; the Secretary of War; the Secretary of the Navy; and the Secretary of Commerce. Except as otherwise provided in this Act, or by other law, the administration of this Act is vested in the Department of State;

(b) The term "United States" when used in a geographical sense, includes the several States and Territories, the insular possessions of the United States (including the Philippine Islands), the Canal Zone, and the District of Columbia;

(c) The term "person" includes a partnership, company, association, or corporation, as well as a natural person.

Within ninety days after the effective date of this Act, or upon first engaging in business, every person who engages in the business of manufacturing, exporting, or importing any of the arms, ammunition, and implements of war referred to in this Act, whether as an exporter, importer, manufacturer, or dealer, shall register with the Secretary of State his name, or business name, principal place of business, and places of business in the United States, and a list of the arms, ammunition, and implements of war which he manufactures, imports, or exports.

Every person required to register under this section shall notify the Secretary of State of any change in the arms, ammunition, and implements of war which he exports, imports, or manufactures; and upon such notification the Secretary of State shall issue to such person an amended certificate of registration, free of charge, which shall remain valid until the date of expiration of the original certificate. Every person required to register under the provisions of this section shall pay a registration fee of $500, and upon receipt of such fee the Secretary of State shall issue a registration certificate valid for five years, which shall be renewable for further periods of five years upon the payment of each renewal of a fee of $500.

It shall be unlawful for any person to export, or attempt to export, from the United States any of the arms, ammunition, or implements of war referred to in this Act to any other country or to import, or attempt to import, to the United States from any other country any of the arms, ammunition, or implements of war referred to in this Act without first having obtained a license therefor.

All persons required to register under this section shall maintain, subject to the inspection of the Board, such permanent records of manufacture for export, importation, and exportation of arms, ammunition, and implements of war as the Board shall prescribe.

Licenses shall be issued to persons who have registered as provided for, except in cases of export or import licenses where exportation of arms, ammunition, or implements of war would be in violation of this Act or any other law of the United States, or of a treaty to which the United States is a party, in which cases such licenses shall not be issued.

The Board shall be called by the Chairman and shall hold at least one meeting a year.

No purchase of arms, ammunition, and implements of war shall be made on behalf of the United States by any officer, executive department, or independent establishment of the Government from any person who shall have failed to register under the provisions of this Act.

The Board shall make an annual report to Congress, copies of which shall be distributed as are other reports transmitted to Congress. Such report shall contain such information and data collected by the Board as may be considered of value in the determination of questions connected with the control of trade in arms, ammunition, and implements of war. It shall include a list of all persons required to register under the provisions of this Act, and full information concerning the licenses issued hereunder.

The Secretary of State shall promulgate such rules and regulations with regard to the enforcement of this section as he may deem necessary to carry out its provisions.

The President is hereby authorized to proclaim upon recommendation of the Board from time to time a list of articles which shall be considered arms, ammunition, and implements of war for the purposes of this section.

This section shall take effect on the ninetieth day after the date of its enactment.

SEC. 3. Whenever the President shall issue the proclamation provided for in section 1 of this Act, thereafter it shall be unlawful for any American vessel to carry any arms, ammunition, or implements of war to any port of the belligerent countries named in such proclamation as being at war, or to any neutral port for transshipment to, or for the use of, a belligerent country.

Whoever, in violation of the provisions of this section, shall take, attempt to take, or shall authorize, hire, or solicit another to take any such vessel carrying such cargo out of port or from the jurisdiction of the United States shall be fined not more than $10,000 or imprisoned not more than five years, or both; and, in addition, such vessel, her tackle, apparel, furniture, equipment, and the arms, ammunition, and implements of war on board shall be forfeited to the United States.

When the President finds the conditions which have caused him to issue his proclamation have ceased to exist, he shall revoke his proclamation, and the provisions of this section shall thereupon cease to apply.

SEC. 4. Whenever, during any war in which the United States is neutral, the President, or any person thereunto authorized by him, shall have cause to believe that any vessel, domestic or foreign, whether requiring clearance or not, is about to carry out of a port of the United States, or its possession, men or fuel, arms, ammunition, implements of war, or other supplies to any warship, tender, or supply ship of a foreign belligerent nation, but the evidence is not deemed sufficient to justify forbidding the departure of the vessel as provided for by section 1, title V, chapter 30, of the Act approved June 15, 1917 (40 Stat.   [2]; U. S. C., title 18, sec. 31), and if, in the President's judgment, such action will serve to maintain peace between the United States and foreign nations, or to protect the commercial interests of the United States and its citizens, or to promote the security of the United States, he shall have the power and it shall be his duty to require the owner, master, or person in command thereof, before departing from a port of the United States, or any of its possessions, for a foreign port, to give a bond to the United States, with sufficient sureties, in such amount as he shall deem proper, conditioned that the vessel will not deliver the men, or the cargo, or any part thereof, to any warship, tender, or supply ship of a belligerent nation; and, if the President, or any person thereunto authorized by him, shall find that a vessel, domestic or foreign, in a port of the United States, or one of its possessions, has previously cleared from such port during such war and delivered its cargo or any part thereof to a warship, tender, or supply ship of a belligerent nation, he may prohibit the departure of such vessel during the duration of the war.

[2] So in original.

SEC. 5. Whenever, during any war in which the United States is neutral, the President shall find that special restrictions placed on the use of the ports and territorial waters of the United States, or of its possessions, by the submarines of a foreign nation will serve to maintain peace between the United States and foreign nations, or to protect the commercial interests of the United States and its citizens, or to promote the security of the United States, and shall make proclamation thereof, it shall thereafter be unlawful for any such submarine to enter a port or the territorial waters of the United States or any of its possessions, or to depart therefrom, except under such conditions and subject to such limitations as the President may prescribe. When, in his judgment, the conditions which have caused him to issue his proclamation have ceased to exist, he shall revoke his proclamation and the provisions of this section shall thereupon cease to apply.

SEC. 6. Whenever, during any war in which the United States is neutral, the President shall find that the maintenance of peace between the United States and foreign nations, or the protection of the lives of citizens of the United States, or the protection of the commercial interests of the United States and its citizens, or the security of the United States requires that the American citizens should refrain from traveling as passengers on the vessels of any belligerent nation, he shall so proclaim, and thereafter no citizen of the United States shall travel on any vessel of any belligerent nation except at his own risk, unless in accordance with such rules and regulations as the President shall prescribe: *Provided, however,* That the provisions of this section shall not apply to a citizen traveling on the vessel of a belligerent whose voyage was begun in advance of the date of the President's proclamation, and who had no opportunity to discontinue his voyage after that date: *And provided further,* That they shall not apply under ninety days after the date of the President's proclamation to a citizen returning from a foreign country to the United States or to any of its possessions. When, in the President's judgment, the conditions which have caused him to issue his proclamation have ceased to exist, he shall revoke his proclamation and the provisions of this section shall thereupon cease to apply.

SEC. 7. In every case of the violation of any of the provisions of this Act where a specific penalty is not herein provided, such violator or violators, upon conviction, shall be fined not more than $10,000 or imprisoned not more than five years, or both.

SEC. 8. If any of the provisions of this Act, or the application thereof to any person or circumstance, is held invalid, the remainder of the Act, and the application of such provision to other persons or circumstances, shall not be affected thereby.

SEC. 9. The sum of $25,000 is hereby authorized to be appropriated, out of any money in the Treasury not otherwise appropriated, to be expended by the Secretary of State in administering this Act.

Approved, August 31, 1935.

APPENDIX 6

PRESIDENT ROOSEVELT'S STATEMENT OF AUGUST 31, 1935 [1]

I have given my approval to S. J. Resolution 173—the neutrality legislation which passed the Congress last week.

I have approved this Joint Resolution because it was intended as an expression of the fixed desire of the Government and the people of the United States to avoid any action which might involve us in war. The purpose is wholly excellent, and this Joint Resolution will to a considerable degree serve that end.

It provides for a licensing system for the control of carrying arms, et cetera, by American vessels; for the control of the use of American waters by foreign submarines; for the restriction of travel by American citizens on vessels of belligerent nations; and for the embargo of the export of arms, et cetera, to both belligerent nations.

The latter section terminates at the end of February 1936. This section requires further and more complete consideration between now and that date. Here again the objective is wholly good. It is the policy of this Government to avoid being drawn into wars between other nations, but it is a fact that no Congress and no Executive can foresee all possible future situations. History is filled with unforeseeable situations that call for some flexibility of action. It is conceivable that situations may arise in which the wholly inflexible provisions of Section I of this Act might have exactly the opposite effect from that which was intended. In other words, the inflexible provisions might drag us into war instead of keeping us out. The policy of the Government is definitely committed to the maintenance of peace and the avoidance of any entanglements which would lead us into conflict. At the same time it is the policy of the

[1] Department of State Press Release.

Government by every peaceful means and without entanglement to coöperate with other similarly minded governments to promote peace.

In several aspects further careful consideration of neutrality needs is most desirable, and there can well be an expansion to include provisions dealing with other important aspects of our neutrality policy which have not been dealt with in this temporary measure.

APPENDIX 7

SECRETARY HULL'S STATEMENT OF SEPTEMBER 12, 1935 [1]

In view of the deep concern of this Government and the widespread anxiety of the American people over recent developments which appear to constitute a grave threat to the peace of the world, I consider it desirable to recapitulate the steps thus far taken by this Government in contributing in every practicable way toward a peaceful settlement of the present dispute between Italy and Ethiopia.

On the evening of July 3 the Emperor of Ethiopia summoned the American Chargé d'Affaires *ad interim* at Addis Ababa to the palace and handed the Chargé a communication in which the Emperor stated that he felt it to be his duty to ask the American Government to examine means of securing observance of the Pact of Paris.

The Chargé was instructed to reply to the Emperor as follows:

I have the honor to acknowledge the receipt of Your Imperial Majesty's note of July 3, 1935, and to inform Your Imperial Majesty that I immediately communicated its contents to my Government. I have been instructed by my Government to reply to your note as follows:

"My Government, interested as it is in the maintenance of peace in all parts of the world, is gratified that the League of Nations, with a view to a peaceful settlement, has given its attention to the controversy which has unhappily arisen between your Government and the Italian Government and that the controversy is now in process of arbitration. My Government hopes that, whatever the facts or merits of the controversy may be, the arbitral agency dealing with this controversy may be able to arrive at a decision satisfactory to both of the Governments immediately concerned.

"Furthermore, and of great importance, in view of the provisions of the Pact of Paris, to which both Italy and Abyssinia

[1] Department of State Press Release.

are parties, in common with sixty-one other countries, my Government would be loath to believe that either of them would resort to other than pacific means as a method of dealing with this controversy or would permit any situation to arise which would be inconsistent with the commitments of the Pact."

On July 10, during a call of the Italian Ambassador made at the request of the Secretary of State, the Secretary made to the Ambassador a statement as follows:

Although we are not familiar with the facts or the merits of the questions at issue between Italy and Ethiopia, we are deeply interested in the preservation of peace in all parts of the world and we are particularly interested in those international arrangements designed to effect the solution of controversies by peaceable means.

Being convinced that world progress and economic recovery are urgently in need of peaceful conditions, particularly at this time, we feel impelled to impress upon the Italian Ambassador our increasing concern over the situation arising out of Italy's dispute with Ethiopia and our earnest hope that a means may be found to arrive at a peaceful and mutually satisfactory solution of the problem.

On July 11, the Secretary of State conferred with the British and French Ambassadors. He called attention to articles which had appeared in the press wherein there was placed upon the American Government's reply to the Emperor of Ethiopia an interpretation implying that the American Government had abandoned the Kellogg-Briand Pact and the pact therefore was "dead."

The Secretary said he felt this interpretation was entirely contrary to the sense of his note to the Emperor, which had emphasized the principles of the Pact of Paris and had given evidence of this Government's interest in the settlement of this dispute by peaceable means.

On the same day, at his press conference, the Secretary of State pointed out that naturally the American Government, as had frequently been stated previously, is deeply concerned about the preservation of peace in every part of the world and is closely observing conditions and developments.

On July 12, in response to various inquiries of newspaper correspondents, the Secretary of State made a statement as follows:

> The Pact of Paris is no less binding now than when it was entered into by the sixty-three nations that are parties to it. By form and designation it constitutes a treaty by and among those nations. It is a declaration by the governments of the world that they condemn recourse to war for the solution of international controversies, and renounce it as an instrument of national policy in their relations with one another. Furthermore, it is an agreement and a solemn obligation that the settlement or solution of all disputes or conflicts among nations, of whatever nature or of whatever origin, shall never be sought except by pacific means.
>
> The United States and the other nations are interested in the maintenance of the pact and the sanctity of the international commitments assumed thereby for the promotion and maintenance of peace among the nations of the world.

On August 1, the President issued a statement as follows:

> At this moment, when the Council of the League of Nations is assembled to consider ways for composing by pacific means the differences that have arisen between Italy and Ethiopia, I wish to voice the hope of the people and the Government of the United States that an amicable solution will be found and that peace will be maintained.

Thereafter, during the month of August, expression of this hope of the people and Government of the United States was communicated in telegrams from the American Government to several other governments.

On September 3, having discovered that an American corporation was a party to a newly granted commercial concession the conclusion of which had added to the perplexities and difficulties confronting the governments and other agencies which are intent upon preservation of peace, the American Government took prompt steps toward removal of this obstacle to peaceful settlement. In connection with that matter, the Secretary of State said at his press conference:

> The central point in the policy of this Government in regard to the Italian and Ethiopian controversy is the preservation of peace—to which policy every country throughout the world is committed by one or more treaties—and we earnestly hope that no nations will, in any circumstances, be diverted from this supreme objective.

Now, this Government feels called upon further to express the attitude of this country.

The Government and people of the United States desire peace. We believe that international controversies can and should be settled by peaceful means. We have signed, along with sixty-two other nations, including Italy and Ethiopia, a treaty in which the signatories have condemned war as an instrument of national policy and have undertaken, each to all, to settle their disputes by none but pacific means.

Under the conditions which prevail in the world today, a threat of hostilities anywhere cannot but be a threat to the interests—political, economic, legal, and social—of all nations. Armed conflict in any part of the world cannot but have undesirable and adverse effects in every part of the world. All nations have the right to ask that any and all issues, between whatsoever nations, be resolved by pacific means. Every nation has the right to ask that no nations subject it and other nations to the hazards and uncertainties that must inevitably accrue to all from resort to arms by any two.

With good will toward all nations, the American Government asks of those countries which appear to be contemplating armed hostilities that they weigh most solicitously the declaration and pledge given in the Pact of Paris, which pledge was entered into by all the signatories for the purpose of safeguarding peace and sparing the world the incalculable losses and human suffering that inevitably attend and follow in the wake of wars.

APPENDIX 8

PRESIDENT ROOSEVELT'S PROCLAMATION OF OCTOBER 5, 1935, CONCERNING THE EXPORT OF ARMS, AMMUNITION, AND IMPLEMENTS OF WAR TO ETHIOPIA AND ITALY [1]

Whereas section 1 of a joint resolution of Congress, entitled "Joint Resolution Providing for the prohibition of the export of arms, ammunition, and implements of war to belligerent countries; the prohibition of the transportation of arms, ammunition, and implements of war by vessels of the United States for the use of belligerent states; for the registration and licensing of persons engaged in the business of manufacturing, exporting, or importing arms, ammunition, or implements of war; and restricting travel by American citizens on belligerent ships during the war," approved August 31, 1935, provides in part as follows:

That upon the outbreak or during the progress of war between, or among, two or more foreign states, the President shall proclaim such fact, and it shall thereafter be unlawful to export arms, ammunition, or implements of war from any place in the United States, or possessions of the United States, to any port of such belligerent states, or to any neutral port for transshipment to, or for the use of, a belligerent country.

And Whereas it is further provided by section 1 of the said joint resolution that

The President, by proclamation, shall definitely enumerate the arms, ammunition, or implements of war, the export of which is prohibited by this Act.

And Whereas it is further provided by section 1 of the said joint resolution that

Whoever in violation of any of the provisions of this section, shall export, or attempt to export, or cause to be exported, arms, ammunition or implements of war from the United States, or any

[1] Department of State Press Release.

of its possessions, shall be fined not more than $10,000 or imprisoned not more than five years, or both, and the property, vessel, or vehicle containing the same shall be subject to the provisions of sections 1 to 8, inclusive, title 6, chapter 30, of the Act approved June 15, 1917 (40 Stat. 223-225; U. S. C. title 22, secs. 238-245).

Now, therefore, I, Franklin D. Roosevelt, President of the United States of America, acting under and by virtue of the authority conferred on me by the said joint resolution of Congress, do hereby proclaim that a state of war unhappily exists between Ethiopia and the Kingdom of Italy; and I do hereby admonish all citizens of the United States or any of its possessions and all persons residing or being within the territory or jurisdiction of the United States or its possessions to abstain from every violation of the provisions of the joint resolution above set forth, hereby made effective and applicable to the export of arms, ammunition, or implements of war from any place in the United States or its possessions to Ethiopia or to the Kingdom of Italy, or to any Italian possession, or to any neutral port for transshipment to, or for the use of, Ethiopia or the Kingdom of Italy.

And I do hereby declare and proclaim that the articles listed below shall be considered arms, ammunition, and implements of war for the purposes of section 1 of the said joint resolution of Congress:

Category I

(1) Rifles and carbines using ammunition in excess of cal. 26.5, and their barrels;

(2) Machine guns, automatic rifles, and machine pistols of all calibers, and their barrels;

(3) Guns, howitzers, and mortars of all calibers, their mountings and barrels;

(4) Ammunition for the arms enumerated under (1) and (2) above, *i.e.*, high-power steel-jacketed ammunition in excess of cal. 26.5; filled and unfilled projectiles and propellants

with a web thickness of .015 inches or greater for the projectiles of the arms enumerated under (3) above;

(5) Grenades, bombs, torpedoes, and mines, filled or unfilled, and apparatus for their use or discharge;

(6) Tanks, military armored vehicles, and armored trains.

Category II

Vessels of war of all kinds, including aircraft carriers and submarines.

Category III

(1) Aircraft, assembled or dismantled, both heavier and lighter than air, which are designed, adapted, and intended for aerial combat by the use of machine guns or of artillery or for the carrying and dropping of bombs or which are equipped with, or which by reason of design or construction are prepared for, any of the appliances referred to in paragraph (2) below;

(2) Aerial gun mounts and frames, bomb racks, torpedo carriers, and bomb or torpedo release mechanisms.

Category IV

Revolvers and automatic pistols of a weight in excess of 1 pound 6 ounces (630 grams), using ammunition in excess of cal. 26.5, and ammunition therefor.

Category V

(1) Aircraft, assembled or dismantled, both heavier and lighter than air, other than those included in category III;

(2) Propellers or air screws, fuselages, hulls, tail units, and under carriage units;

(3) Aircraft engines.

Appendix 8

Category VI

(1) Livens projectors and flame throwers;
(2) Mustard gas, lewisite, ethyldichlorarsine, and methyldichlorarsine.

And I do hereby enjoin upon all officers of the United States, charged with the execution of the laws thereof, the utmost diligence in preventing violations of the said joint resolution, and this my proclamation issued thereunder, and in bringing to trial and punishment any offenders against the same.

And I do hereby delegate to the Secretary of State the power of prescribing regulations for the enforcement of section 1 of the said joint resolution of August 31, 1935, as made effective by this my proclamation issued thereunder.

IN WITNESS WHEREOF, I have hereunto set my hand and caused the seal of the United States to be affixed.

DONE at the City of Washington this 5th day of October, in the year of our Lord nineteen hundred and thirty-five, and of the Independence of the United States of America the one hundred and sixtieth.

FRANKLIN D. ROOSEVELT.

By the President:
CORDELL HULL,
Secretary of State.

APPENDIX 9

PRESIDENT ROOSEVELT'S PROCLAMATION OF OCTOBER 5, 1935, CONCERNING TRAVEL BY AMERICAN CITIZENS ON VESSELS OF BELLIGERENT NATIONS [1]

Whereas Section 6 of the Joint Resolution of Congress, approved August 31, 1935 (Public Resolution No. 67—74th Congress), provides that

Whenever, during any war in which the United States is neutral, the President shall find that the maintenance of peace between the United States and foreign nations, or the protection of the lives of citizens of the United States, or the protection of the commercial interests of the United States and its citizens, or the security of the United States requires that the American citizens should refrain from traveling as passengers on the vessels of any belligerent nation, he shall so proclaim, and thereafter no citizen of the United States shall travel on any vessel of any belligerent nation except at his own risk, unless in accordance with such rules and regulations as the President shall prescribe: *Provided, however,* That the provisions of this section shall not apply to a citizen traveling on the vessel of a belligerent whose voyage was begun in advance of the date of the President's proclamation, and who had no opportunity to discontinue his voyage after that date: *And provided further,* That they shall not apply under ninety days after the date of the President's proclamation to a citizen returning from a foreign country to the United States or to any of its possessions. When, in the President's judgment, the conditions which have caused him to issue his proclamation have ceased to exist, he shall revoke his proclamation and the provisions of this section shall thereupon cease to apply.

And Whereas war now unhappily exists between Ethiopia and the Kingdom of Italy; and

Whereas I find that the protection of the lives of citizens of the United States requires that American citizens should refrain from traveling as passengers on the vessels of either of the belligerent nations;

[1] Department of State Press Release.

Now, therefore, I, Franklin D. Roosevelt, President of the United States of America, acting under and by virtue of the authority vested in me by the said Joint Resolution of Congress, do hereby admonish all citizens of the United States to abstain from traveling on any vessel of either of the belligerent nations contrary to the provisions of the said Joint Resolution; and

I do hereby give notice that any citizen of the United States who may travel on such a vessel, contrary to the provisions of the said Joint Resolution, will do so at his own risk.

In witness whereof, I have hereunto set my hand and caused the seal of the United States to be affixed.

DONE at the city of Washington this fifth day of October, in the year of our Lord nineteen hundred and thirty-five, and of the Independence of the United States of America the one hundred and sixtieth.

FRANKLIN D. ROOSEVELT.

By the President:
 CORDELL HULL,
  Secretary of State.

APPENDIX 10

A NOTE ON PREVIOUS AMERICAN EMBARGOES OF ARMS SHIPMENTS

Arms embargoes have been employed by the United States Government mainly as a means of promoting political stability in neighboring republics. President Theodore Roosevelt established a precedent for such action in 1905. He based his authority on a Joint Resolution of April 22, 1898, enacted during the Spanish-American War and authorizing the President "in his discretion, and with such limitations and exceptions as to himself may seem expedient, to prohibit the export of coal and other material used in war from any seaport of the United States until otherwise ordered by Congress."[1]

The original object of this legislation was to prevent military supplies from being shipped from the United States to places where they might become available to Spanish forces in the Caribbean; but President Roosevelt found the measure useful for another purpose. In response to the appeal of President Morales of the Dominican Republic, he established a financial receivership for that country in order to relieve its government of the pressure of foreign creditors whose procedure incidentally threatened to impinge upon the Monroe Doctrine. To prevent these financial arrangements from being upset by revolution in the Dominican Republic, President Roosevelt utilized his powers under the war legislation of 1898 and forbade the "export of arms, ammunition and munitions of war of every kind" to that country.

The authority which Mr. Roosevelt thus exercised was made more specific by new legislation in 1912, when Congress also repealed the embargo measure of 1898. A Joint Resolution of March 14 empowered the President to prohibit

---

[1] 30 U. S. Statutes, 339. See also *Congressional Record*, Seventy-third Congress, First Session, 1743.

the exportation of arms or munitions of war to any American country in which there were "conditions of domestic violence," and where such conditions might be aggravated "by the use of arms or munitions of war procured from the United States." By a second Joint Resolution of January 31, 1922, the President's power was extended to countries in which the United States exercised extraterritorial jurisdiction—specifically, to China.

Immediately after his approval of the Joint Resolution of 1912, President Taft imposed an embargo on shipments of arms to Mexico because of the revolutionary disturbances in that country. In 1914, President Wilson lifted the embargo in order that shipments might reach the Carranza government, which he was disposed to favor in preference to the government of Huerta. The Carranza government in northern Mexico was cut off by its opponents from access to the sea and could obtain military supplies only from the United States, while the Huerta government could import arms and munitions from Europe. The embargo on shipments to Mexico was re-employed in 1915, 1919 and 1924. On March 4, 1922, President Harding issued a proclamation extending the embargo to China. Similar proclamations, which were still in effect in 1935, were issued with respect to Honduras on March 22, 1924; with respect to Nicaragua on September 15, 1926; and with respect to Cuba on June 29, 1934. Under these provisions the exportation of arms to China, Cuba, Honduras and Nicaragua is permitted only when the Department of State has been informed by the diplomatic representatives of these countries that such shipments are desired by the governments of the respective countries.

On May 28, 1934, Congress passed a Joint Resolution authorizing the President to prohibit the sale of arms and munitions of war "to those countries now engaged in armed conflict in the Chaco," namely Bolivia and Paraguay. On the same day, President Franklin D. Roosevelt issued a proclamation making effective an embargo on arms shipments to these countries. This embargo remained in effect until November 29, when it was lifted because the war in the Chaco was officially ended.

The United States Government has usually employed its arms embargo in the case of revolutions in Latin American countries with a view to aiding one of the parties or ending a war rather than with a view to maintaining strict impartiality between the disputants. Following the precedent established by President Wilson in 1914, President Coolidge in 1926 allowed the adherents of the Diaz government in Nicaragua to obtain munitions in the United States while withholding them from the opponents of the Diaz régime. On several occasions, notably in 1924 and 1929, the United States has sold arms to the existing government in Mexico when it was threatened with revolution.

Early in 1933 an effort was made in Congress to give the President authority to declare an embargo on arms shipments to any country where such shipments might promote "the employment of force in the course of a dispute or conflict between nations." A Joint Resolution to this effect passed the Senate on January 19, 1933, but the House failed to act before Congress adjourned. When the new Congress convened in special session the House passed the resolution on April 17 by a vote of 253 to 109. In the Senate, however, the resolution was amended so as to make the embargo apply impartially to all the disputants. The Administration made no effort to obtain the passage of the measure in this form.

W. O. S.

APPENDIX 11—KEY WAR MATERIALS
PERCENTAGES OF WORLD PRODUCTION, 1929, BY COUNTRIES [1]

	United States	Great Britain	Canada	S. Africa	Australia	Br. India	Malay States	Other British	Germany	France	Russia	Italy	Belgium	Belg. Congo	Norway	Sweden	Switzerland	Greece	Hungary	Jugoslavia	Spain	D. E. Indies	Siam	China	Japan	Mexico	Cuba	Argentina	Bolivia	Brazil	Chile	Dutch Guiana	Peru	Venezuela	All other
Minerals																																			
Aluminum	39	5	11	..	..	..	..	..	12	11	..	3	..	..	10	..	8	..	..	..	..	..	..	..	2	..	..	..	..	..	..	..	..	..	1
Bauxite	17	..	..	..	..	..	..	9	..	31	..	9	..	..	..	..	..	..	18	5	..	..	..	..	4	..	..	..	..	..	..	10	..	..	1
Chromite	..	..	..	11	..	9	..	44	..	..	5	..	..	..	..	..	..	4	..	7	2	..	..	..	..	..	..	..	..	..	..	..	..	..	9
Copper	54	7	4	..	3	1	..	..	3	..	1	..	..	7	..	..	..	..	..	..	3	..	..	..	..	3	9	..	..	..	16	..	3	..	3
Iron Ore	37	7	..	..	..	1	..	15	3	25	4	..	..	..	..	6	..	..	..	..	..	..	..	..	4	..	..	..	..	..	..	..	..	..	14
Pig Iron	44	8	1	..	1	1	..	16	15	11	4	..	4	..	..	..	..	..	..	..	..	..	..	..	..	..	..	..	..	..	..	..	..	..	12
Steel	48	8	1	..	..	..	..	..	16	8	4	..	3	..	..	..	..	..	..	..	..	..	..	..	..	..	..	..	..	..	..	..	..	..	12
Lead	36	..	8	..	10	5	..	..	5	1	..	1	5	..	..	..	..	..	..	..	8	..	..	..	..	13	..	..	..	..	..	..	..	..	8
Manganese	2	..	..	..	..	29	..	19	..	..	34	..	..	..	..	..	..	..	..	..	..	..	..	..	..	..	..	..	..	9	..	..	..	..	7
Nickel	..	..	90	..	..	..	..	..	..	..	..	..	..	..	..	..	..	..	..	..	..	..	..	..	..	..	..	..	..	..	..	..	..	..	10
Nitrates (nat.)	..	..	..	..	..	..	..	..	..	..	..	..	..	..	..	..	..	..	..	..	..	..	..	..	..	..	..	..	..	..	100	..	..	..	..
Potash	2	..	..	..	..	..	..	..	74	20	..	..	..	..	..	..	..	..	..	..	1	..	..	..	..	..	..	..	..	..	..	..	..	..	3
Petroleum	68	..	..	..	..	..	..	..	..	..	7	..	..	..	..	..	..	..	..	..	..	3	..	..	..	3	..	..	..	..	..	..	1	9	9
Tin	..	..	..	..	..	..	38	6	..	..	..	..	..	..	..	..	..	..	..	..	..	17	4	4	..	..	..	..	25	..	..	..	..	..	6
Tungsten	4	..	..	..	..	20	7	..	..	..	..	..	..	..	..	..	..	..	..	..	..	..	..	55	..	..	..	..	5	..	..	..	..	..	9
Vanadium	17	..	..	..	..	..	20	..	..	..	..	..	..	..	..	..	..	..	..	..	..	..	..	..	..	..	..	..	..	..	..	..	59	..	4
Other Key Materials																																			
Cotton	56	..	..	..	..	16	..	7	..	..	4	..	..	..	..	..	..	..	..	..	..	..	..	8	..	..	..	..	..	..	..	..	..	..	9
Rubber	1	..	..	..	3	8	53	13	..	..	..	..	..	..	..	..	..	..	..	..	..	29	..	..	..	..	..	..	..	..	..	..	..	..	4
Wheat	19	..	7	..	3	8	..	1	..	8	16	6	..	..	..	..	..	..	2	2	..	..	..	..	..	..	..	4	..	..	..	..	..	..	20

[1] The year 1929 has been selected for this exhibit, since the production of most key commodities in more recent years has been subnormal and hence does not indicate potential output under war conditions. Since 1929 new fields of production have developed for several commodities, notably for copper in Northern Rhodesia and for cotton in Brazil. (Sources: "Mineral Resources of the United States, 1930," v. I and II; League of Nations "Statistical Yearbook," 1930–31; William Rawles, "The Nationality of Commercial Control of World Minerals.")

APPENDIX 12

CHANGES IN AMERICAN EXPORT TRADE, 1913-1934 [1]

	Wheat and Flour [2] (1,000 bus.)	Cotton, incl. Linters (1,000 bales)	Crude Foodstuffs (in $1,000)	Finished Mfrs. (in $1,000)
1913	154,768	8,544	181,907	776,297
1914	231,324	6,084	137,495	724,908
1928	206,258	7,542	294,677	2,260,002
1929	163,688	8,044	269,590	2,531,823
1930	153,247	6,690	178,533	1,898,089
1931	131,477	6,760	127,072	1,119,657
1932	135,799	8,708	89,419	642,228
1933	41,211	8,419	48,366	616,639
1934	36,436	5,942	59,285	878,987

[1] Source, "Statistical Abstract of the United States."
[2] Flour converted to grain at rate of 4.7 bushels to barrel.

APPENDIX 13

AMERICAN EXPORTS OF CERTAIN WAR MATERIALS TO ITALY, 1934-1935 [1]

	Iron and Steel Scrap (tons)		Crude Petroleum (barrels)		Gasoline (barrels)		Fuel Oils (barrels)	
	1934	1935	1934	1935	1934	1935	1934	1935
Jan.	6,560	20,425	......	62,039	3	72,997	56,007	120,486
Feb.	2,466	33,269	72,630	......	4	27,625	70,608	......
Mar.	31,403	27,783	59,236	......	......	1	61,690	59,013
Apr.	10,879	8,447	153,997	......	......	......	......	53,565
May	17,314	26,366	74,875	......	......	14,625	......	......
June	25,686	26,271	84,798	......	......	12,412	63,356	119,885
July	21,803	62,169	......	61,853	6	2,013	60,410	76,271
Aug.	21,068	33,078	......	88,656	12,273	30,639	......	119,092
Sept.	21,066	40,432	......	61,708	1	......	53,204	84,349
Oct.	18,021	44,301	......	417,474	......	......	......	22,822
Nov.	22,453	25,065	......	316,955	49,534	78,284	......	158,503
Total	198,719	347,606	445,536	1,008,685	61,821	238,596	365,275	813,986

[1] Source, U. S. Department of Commerce.

ADDENDUM 1

DRAFT NEUTRALITY BILL, INTRODUCED JANUARY 3, 1936, BY SENATOR PITTMAN [1]

Be it enacted by the Senate and House of Representatives of the United States of America in Congress assembled, That this Act may be cited as the "Neutrality Act of 1936."

Definitions

SEC. 2. For the purposes of this Act—

(a) The term "Board" means the National Munitions Control Board.

(b) The term "United States" when used in a geographical sense means the continental United States, the Territories and insular possessions of the United States (including the Philippine Islands), the Canal Zone, and the District of Columbia.

(c) The term "person" means a natural person, corporation, partnership, organization, or association.

(d) The term "vessel" means every description of watercraft (including aircraft) or other contrivance used, or capable of being used, as a means of transportation on or over water.

(e) The term "American vessel" means any vessel (including aircraft) documented under the laws of the United States.

(f) The term "vehicle" means every description of carriage (including aircraft) or other contrivance used, or capable of being used, as a means of transportation on or over land.

Export of Arms, Ammunition, and Implements of War

SEC. 3. (a) Upon the outbreak or during the progress of any war between, or among, two or more foreign states, the President shall proclaim such fact, and it shall thereafter

---

[1] S. 3474, 74th Congress, 2d Session. On the same date a similar bill was introduced in the House by Mr. McReynolds as H. J. Res. 422. This projected legislation was laid aside in favor of the Joint Resolution appearing on p. 179.

be unlawful to export, or attempt to export, or cause to be exported, or sell for export, arms, ammunition, or implements of war from any place in the United States to any belligerent country, named in the proclamation, or to any neutral country for transshipment to or for the use of any such belligerent country.

(b) The President shall, by proclamation, definitely enumerate the arms, ammunition, and implements of war, the export of which is prohibited by this Act.

(c) The President shall, from time to time, by proclamation, extend such embargo upon the export of arms, ammunition, and implements of war to other countries as and when they may become involved in such war.

(d) When in the judgment of the President the conditions which have caused him to issue a proclamation have ceased to exist, he shall revoke the same and the provisions of this section shall thereupon cease to apply.

Export of Articles and Materials Used for War Purposes

SEC. 4. (a) Whenever during any war in which the United States is neutral, the President shall find that the placing of restrictions on the shipment from the United States to belligerent countries of certain articles or materials used in the manufacture of arms, ammunition, or implements of war, or in the conduct of war, will serve to promote the security and preserve the neutrality of the United States, or to protect the lives and commerce of nationals of the United States, or that to refrain from placing such restrictions would contribute to a prolongation or expansion of the war he shall so proclaim, and it shall thereafter be unlawful to export, or attempt to export, or cause to be exported, or sell for export, such articles or materials from any place in the United States to any belligerent country named in the proclamation, or to any neutral country for transshipment to or for the use of any such belligerent country in excess of a normal amount, in quantity and kind, of exports from the United States to the respective belligerent countries prior to the date of the proclamation, such normal amount to constitute the average of shipments during a previous period of years to be determined by the President: *Provided,* That no restriction or prohibition imposed under this section shall under any circumstances be applied to food or medical supplies.

(b) The President shall, by proclamation, definitely enumerate the articles or materials the exportation of which is to be restricted, and he may, from time to time, modify or revoke in whole or in part any proclamation issued by him under this section when he shall find that the conditions which caused him to issue his proclamation have ceased to exist or have so changed as to justify in his opinion such modification or revocation.

(c) The President shall, from time to time, by proclamation, extend such restrictions as are imposed under this section to other countries as and when they may become involved in such war.

Financial Transactions with Belligerent Governments

SEC. 5. (a) Whenever the President shall have issued his proclamation as provided for in section 2 of this Act, it shall thereafter during the period of the war be unlawful for any person within the United States to purchase or sell bonds, securities, or other obligations of the government of any belligerent country, or of any political subdivision thereof, or of any person acting for or on behalf of such government, issued after the date of such proclamation, or to make any loan or extend any credit to any such government or person: *Provided,* That if the President shall find that such action will serve to protect the commercial or other interests of the United States or its nationals, he may, in his discretion, and to such extent and under such regulations as he may prescribe, except from the operation of this section ordinary commercial credits and short-time obligations in aid of legal transactions and of a character customarily used in current commercial business.

(b) The provisions of this section shall not apply to a renewal or adjustment of indebtedness existing on the date of the President's proclamation.

(c) Whoever shall violate the provisions of this section or of any regulations issued hereunder shall, upon conviction thereof, be fined not more than $10,000 or imprisoned for not more than five years, or both. Should the violation be by a corporation, organization, or association, any officer or agent thereof participating in the violation shall be liable to the penalty herein prescribed.

(d) When the President shall have revoked his proclamation as provided for in section 2 of this Act, the provisions of this section and of any regulations issued by the President hereunder shall thereupon cease to apply.

Equal Application of Embargoes, and so forth

SEC. 6. Any embargo, prohibition, or restriction that may be imposed by or under the provisions of sections 2, 3, or 4 of this Act shall apply equally to all belligerents, unless the Congress, with the approval of the President, shall declare otherwise.

American Vessels Prohibited from Carrying Arms, and so forth

SEC. 7. (a) Whenever the President shall have issued a proclamation as provided for in section 2 of this Act it shall thereafter be unlawful for any American vessel to carry arms, ammunition, or implements of war to any belligerent country named therein, or to any neutral country for transshipment to, or for the use of, such belligerent country.

(b) If the President shall find that the maintenance of peace between the United States and foreign nations, or the protection of the commercial interests of the United States and its nationals, or the security or neutrality of the United States would be promoted by prohibiting American vessels from carrying any of the articles or materials enumerated in any proclamation issued by him under section 3 of this Act, and shall so proclaim, it shall thereafter be unlawful for any

American vessel to carry any such articles or materials from any place in the United States to any belligerent country or to any neutral country for transshipment to or for the use of any belligerent country.

(c) The President may, from time to time, modify or revoke in whole or in part any proclamation issued by him under paragraph (b) of this section.

(d) When in the judgment of the President the conditions which have caused him to issue his proclamation have ceased to exist, he shall revoke the same and the provisions of this section shall thereupon cease to apply.

Penalties for Violation of Section 2, 3, or 6

SEC. 8. (a) Whoever, in violation of any of the provisions of section 2, 3, or 6 of this Act, shall export, or attempt to export, or cause to be exported, or sell for export, arms, ammunition, implements of war, or other articles or materials enumerated in a proclamation by the President, or shall take, attempt to take, or shall authorize, hire, or solicit another to take any vessel or vehicle carrying such cargo out of a port or from the jurisdiction of the United States, shall be fined not more than $10,000 or imprisoned not more than five years, or both; and, in addition, such vessel or vehicle, her tackle, apparel, furniture, equipment, and such part of the property or cargo as is covered by the proclamation shall be subject to the provisions of sections 1 to 8, inclusive, title 6, chapter 30, of the Act approved June 15, 1917 (40 Stat. 223-225; U. S. C., title 22, secs. 238-245).

(b) In the case of the forfeiture of any arms, ammunition, or implements of war, by reason of a violation of this Act, no public or private sale shall be required, but such arms, ammunition, or implements of war shall be delivered to the Secretary of War for such use or disposal thereof as shall be approved by the President.

Transactions with Belligerents

SEC. 9. Whenever, during any war in which the United States is neutral, the President shall find that the maintenance of peace between the United States and foreign nations, or the protection of the commercial interests of the United States and its nationals, or the security or neutrality of the United States would be promoted by requiring nationals of the United States to assume the risk of commercial transactions with the governments or nationals of belligerent countries, or persons residing therein, and shall so proclaim, thereafter American nationals who engage in such transactions shall do so at their own risk.

Travel by American Nationals on Belligerent Vessels

SEC. 10. (a) Whenever the President shall have issued his proclamation as provided for in section 2 of this Act, thereafter no national of the United States shall travel on any vessel of any belligerent nation except at his own risk, unless in accordance with such rules and regulations as the President shall prescribe. No passport issued by the Secretary of State or anyone acting under his authority shall be valid for use by any person for travel from the United States on any such vessel.

(b) The provisions of this section shall not apply to a national whose voyage on a vessel of a belligerent was begun in advance of the date on the President's proclamation, and who had no opportunity to discontinue the voyage after that date; nor shall they apply under ninety days after the date of the President's proclamation to a national returning from a foreign country to the United States.

(c) When the President shall have revoked his proclamation as provided for in section 2 of this Act, the provisions of this section and of any regulations issued by the President hereunder shall thereupon cease to apply.

Use of American Ports as Base of Supply

SEC. 11. (a) Whenever, during any war in which the United States is neutral, the President, or any person thereunto authorized by him, shall have cause to believe that any vessel, domestic or foreign, whether requiring clearance or not, is about to carry out of a port of the United States fuel, arms, ammunition, men, supplies, dispatches, or information to any warship, tender, or supply ship of a belligerent nation, but the evidence is not deemed sufficient to justify forbidding the departure of the vessel as provided for by section 1, title V, chapter 30, of the Act approved June 15, 1917 (40 Stat. 217, 221; U. S. C., title 18, sec. 31), and if, in the President's judgment, such action will serve to maintain peace between the United States and foreign nations, or to protect the commercial interests of the United States and its nationals, or to promote the security or neutrality of the United States, he shall have the power and it shall be his duty to require the owner, master, or person in command thereof, before departing from a port of the United States to give a bond to the United States, with sufficient sureties, in such amount as he shall deem proper, conditioned that the vessel will not deliver the men, dispatches, information, or any part of the cargo, to any warship, tender, or supply ship of a belligerent nation.

(b) If the President, or any person thereunto authorized by him, shall find that a vessel, domestic or foreign, in a port of the United States, has previously cleared from a port of the United States during such war and delivered its cargo or any part thereof to a warship, tender, or supply ship of a belligerent nation, he may prohibit the departure of such vessel during the duration of the war.

Submarines Prohibited from Entering American Waters

SEC. 12. (a) Whenever, during any war in which the United States is neutral, the President shall find that the placing of special restrictions on the use of the ports and territorial waters of the United States by submarines of belligerent nations will serve to maintain peace between the United States and foreign nations, or to protect the commercial interests of the United States and its nationals, or to promote the security or neutrality of the United States, and shall so proclaim, it shall thereafter be unlawful for any such submarine to enter a port or the territorial waters of the United States, or to depart therefrom, except under such conditions and subject to such limitations as the President may prescribe.

(b) When, in the judgment of the President, the conditions which have caused him to issue his proclamation have ceased to exist, he shall revoke the same and the provisions of this section shall thereupon cease to apply.

National Munitions Control Board

SEC. 13. Section 2 of the joint resolution (Public Resolution Numbered 67, Seventy-fourth Congress), approved August 31, 1935, is hereby amended to read as follows:

"(a) The National Munitions Control Board which is hereby established shall consist of the Secretary of State, who shall be chairman and executive officer of the Board, the Secretary of the Treasury, the Secretary of War, the Secretary of the Navy, and the Secretary of Commerce. Except as otherwise provided in this section or by other law, the administration of this section is vested in the Department of State.

"(b) The President is hereby authorized to proclaim upon recommendation of the Board from time to time a list of articles which shall be considered arms, ammunition, and implements of war for the purposes of this section.

"(c) Every person who engages in the business of manufacturing for export, exporting, or importing any of the arms, ammunition, or implements of war referred to in paragraph (b) of this section, whether as an exporter, importer, manufacturer, or dealer, shall register with the Secretary of State his name, or style, principal place of business, and places of business in the United States, and a list of the arms, ammunition, and implements of war which he exports, imports, or manufactures for export.

"(d) Every person required to register under the provisions of this section shall pay a registration fee of $500 and upon receipt of such fee the Secretary of State shall issue a registration certificate valid for five years which shall be renewable for further periods of five years upon the payment for each renewal of a fee of $500.

"(e) Every person required to register under this section shall notify the Secretary of State of any change in the arms, ammunition, or implements of war which he exports, imports, or manufactures for export; and upon such notification the Secretary of

State shall issue to such person an amended certificate of registration, free of charge, which shall remain valid until the date of expiration of the original certificate.

"(f) It shall be unlawful for any person required to register under the provisions of this section to import or export any of the arms, ammunition, or implements of war referred to in paragraph (b) of this section without having registered in accordance with the provisions of this section.

"(g) It shall be unlawful for any person to export, or attempt to export, from the United States any of the arms, ammunition, or implements of war referred to in paragraph (b) of this section to any other country, or to import, or attempt to import, to the United States from any other country any of the arms, ammunition, or implements of war referred to in said paragraph (b), without first having obtained a license therefor from the Department of State for each shipment.

"(h) Export and import licenses shall be issued to persons who have registered as herein provided for, except in cases where the exportation of arms, ammunition, or implements of war would be in violation of this section or any other law of the United States, or of a treaty to which the United States is a party, in which cases such licenses shall not be issued: *Provided, however,* That after the ninetieth day following the effective date of this Act no export licenses shall be issued unless the government of the country to which such arms are to be exported has indicated to the satisfaction of the Secretary of State that permission for the importation has been accorded: *And provided further,* That after the ninetieth day following the effective date of this Act no licenses shall be issued for the export of appliances and substances exclusively intended for chemical warfare.

"(i) The Secretary of State shall issue regulations for carrying out the provisions of this section.

"(j) The Board shall be called into session by the chairman and shall hold at least one meeting a year.

"(k) No purchase of arms, ammunition, or implements of war shall be made on behalf of the United States by any officer, executive department, or independent establishment of the Government from any person who shall have failed to register under the provisions of paragraph (c) of this section.

"(l) Any contract in violation of the provisions of paragraph (k) of this section is hereby declared to be contrary to the public policy of the United States, shall not be enforceable in any court of the United States, and shall not afford any basis for the granting of legal or equitable relief by any such court.

"(m) No sale of the arms, ammunition, or implements of war referred to in paragraph (b) of this section shall be made on behalf of the United States by any officer, executive department, or independent establishment of the Government to any foreign government on or after November 29, 1936. The provisions of the Act of August 29, 1916, relating to the sale of ordnance and stores to the Government of Cuba (39 Stat. 619, 643; U. S. C., title 50, sec. 72), are hereby abrogated as of November 29, 1936.

"(n) All persons required to register under this section shall maintain, subject to the inspection of the Secretary of State, such permanent records of manufacture for export, importation, and exportation of arms, ammunition, and implements of war as he shall prescribe.

"(o) Any person who violates or fails to comply with any of the requirements of this section or any regulations issued under this section shall, on conviction, be fined not more than $10,000 or be imprisoned for not more than five years, or both, in the discretion of the court.

"(p) The Board shall make an annual report to Congress, copies of which shall be distributed as are other reports transmitted to Congress. Such report shall contain such information and data collected by the Board as may be considered of value in the determination of questions in connection with the control of trade in arms, ammunition, and implements of war. It shall include a list of all persons required to register under the provisions of this section and full information concerning the licenses issued under the provisions of this section.

"(q) Such amount as may from time to time be deemed necessary is hereby authorized to be appropriated, out of any money in the Treasury not otherwise appropriated, to be expended by the Secretary of State in carrying out the duties as aforesaid and in defraying the expenses of the Board in discharging the duties placed upon it by this section."

Regulations by the President

SEC. 14. The President may, from time to time, promulgate such rules and regulations, not inconsistent with law, as may be necessary and proper to carry out any of the provisions of this Act; and he may exercise any power or authority conferred on him by this Act through such officer or officers, or agency or agencies, as he shall direct.

Application of Provisions of This Act

Sec. 15. If any of the provisions of this Act, or the application thereof to any person or circumstance, is held invalid, the remainder of the Act, and the application of such provision to other persons or circumstances, shall not be affected thereby.

Modification or Termination of Treaties

Sec. 16. (a) If the President shall find that any of the provisions of this Act, if applied, would contravene treaty provisions in force between the United States and any foreign country, he may enter into negotiations with the government of such country for the purpose of effecting such modification of the treaty provisions as may be necessary, and if he shall be unable to bring about the necessary modifications, he may, in his discretion, give notice of termination of the treaty.

(b) Except to the extent that the law and rules of neutrality are or may be temporarily or provisionally modified by or under authority of this Act, the United States reserves and reaffirms its rights under international law as it existed prior to August 1, 1914.

Repeal of Joint Resolution of August 31, 1935

Sec. 17. Section 1 and sections 3 to 9, inclusive, of the joint resolution (Public Resolution Numbered 67, Seventy-fourth Congress) approved August 31, 1935, are hereby repealed, but such repeal shall not affect any proclamation issued by the President pursuant to that resolution. Any such proclamation shall remain effective until revoked in accordance with the corresponding provisions of the present Act.

Authorization for Appropriations

Sec. 18. There is hereby authorized to be appropriated from time to time, out of any money in the Treasury not otherwise appropriated, such amounts as may be necessary to carry out the provisions and accomplish the purposes of this Act.

ADDENDUM 2

JOINT RESOLUTION EXTENDING AND AMENDING THE NEUTRALITY ACT OF AUGUST 31, 1935 [1]

Resolved by the Senate and House of Representatives of the United States of America in Congress assembled, That section 1 of the joint resolution (Public Res. No. 67, 74th Cong.), approved August 31, 1935, be, and the same hereby is, amended by striking out in the first section, on the second line, after the word "assembled" the following words: "That upon the outbreak or during the progress of war between," and inserting therefor the words: "Whenever the President shall find that there exists a state of war between;" and by striking out the word "may" after the word "President" and before the word "from" in the twelfth line, and inserting in lieu thereof the word "shall"; and by substituting for the last paragraph of said section the following paragraph: "except with respect to offenses committed, or forfeitures incurred prior to May 1, 1937, this section and all proclamations issued thereunder shall not be effective after May 1, 1937."

SEC. 2. There are hereby added to said joint resolution two new sections, to be known as sections 1a and 1b, reading as follows:

"SEC. 1a. Whenever the President shall have issued his proclamation as provided for in secton 1 of this Act, it shall thereafter during the period of the war be unlawful for any person within the United States to purchase, sell, or exchange bonds, securities, or other obligations of the government of any belligerent country, or of any political subdivision thereof, or of any person acting for or on behalf of such government, issued after the date of such proclamation, or to make any loan or extend any credit to any such government or person: *Provided,* That if the President shall find that

---

[1] H. J. Res. 491, 74th Congress, 2d Session. Passed by the House of Representatives February 17, 1936, and by the Senate February 18; signed by President Roosevelt February 29, 1936.

such action will serve to protect the commercial or other interests of the United States or its nationals, he may, in his discretion, and to such extent and under such regulation as he may prescribe, except from the operation of this section ordinary commercial credits and short-time obligations in aid of legal transactions and of a character customarily used in normal peace-time commercial transactions.

"The provisions of this section shall not apply to a renewal or adjustment of such indebtedness as may exist on the date of the President's proclamation.

"Whoever shall violate the provisions of this section or of any regulations issued hereunder shall, upon conviction thereof, be fined not more than $50,000 or imprisoned for not more than 5 years, or both. Should the violation be by a corporation, organization, or association, each officer or agent thereof participating in the violation may be liable to the penalty herein prescribed.

"When the President shall have revoked his proclamation as provided for in section 1 of this Act, the provisions of this section and of any regulations issued by the President hereunder shall thereupon cease to apply.

"SEC. 1b. This Act shall not apply to an American republic or republics engaged in war against a non-American state or states, provided the American republic is not cooperating with a non-American state or states in such war."

SEC. 3. Section 9 of said joint resolution is amended to read as follows:

"There is hereby authorized to be appropriated from time to time, out of any money in the Treasury not otherwise appropriated, such amounts as may be necessary to carry out the provisions and accomplish the purposes of this Act."

BIBLIOGRAPHY ON AMERICAN NEUTRALITY
GENERAL, HISTORICAL AND LEGAL

Books:

ADAMS, HENRY. History of the United States. New edition. New York, Scribners, 1921, 9v.

BEMIS, GEORGE. American Neutrality: Its Honorable Past, Its Expedient Future. Boston, Little, Brown, 1866, 211p.

BEMIS, SAMUEL FLAGG. Diplomacy of the American Revolution. New York, Appleton-Century, 1935, 293p. (Foundations of American Diplomacy, 1775-1823, V. I.)

CRECRAFT, EARL W. Freedom of the Seas. New York, Appleton-Century, 1935, 304p.

FENWICK, CHARLES G. Neutrality Laws of the United States. Washington, Carnegie Endowment for International Peace, 1913, 200p.

HYDE, CHARLES C. International Law, Chiefly as Interpreted and Applied by the United States. Boston, Little, Brown, 1922, 2v.

HYNEMAN, CHARLES S. First American Neutrality. Urbana, University of Illinois, 1934, 178p.

MAHAN, ALFRED THAYER. Sea Power in Its Relations to the War of 1812. Boston, Little, Brown, 1919, 2v.

MOORE, JOHN BASSETT. Digest of International Law. Washington, Government Printing Office, 1906, 8v.

—————. International Law and Some Current Illusions. New York, Macmillan, 1924, 381p.

—————. The Principles of American Diplomacy. New York, Harper, 1918.

Neutrality: Its History, Economics and Law. New York, Columbia University Press, 1935, 4v. (Only V. I "The Origins" by Philip C. Jessup and Francis Deák has appeared to date. Volumes to follow: V. II. "The Napoleonic Period." V. III. "The World War Period." V. IV. "Today and Tomorrow.")

OPPENHEIM, L. F. L. International Law. New York, Longmans, 5th Edition, 1935, 2v.

SAVAGE, CARLTON. Policy of the United States toward Maritime Commerce in War; V. I: 1776-1914. Washington, Government Printing Office, 1934, 533p.

SCOTT, JAMES BROWN, ed. The Controversy over Neutral Rights between the United States and France, 1797-1800. New York, Oxford, 1917, 510p.

SEARS, LOUIS MARTIN. Jefferson and the Embargo. Durham, N. C., Duke University Press, 1927, 340p.

THOMAS, CHARLES M. American Neutrality in 1793. New York, Columbia University Press, 1931, 295p.

U. S. LAWS, STATUTES, ETC. The Laws of Neutrality as Existing on August 1, 1914. Washington, Government Printing Office, 1918, 578p.

WRIGHT, QUINCY. The Future of Neutrality.... New York, Carnegie Endowment for International Peace, 98p. (*International Conciliation*, September, 1928, No. 242.)

WORLD WAR PERIOD

Books:

BAKER, RAY STANNARD and DODD, W. E., eds. Public Papers of Woodrow Wilson. New York, Harper, 1926, V. 3-4.

BAKER, RAY STANNARD. Woodrow Wilson, Life and Letters; V. 5, Neutrality, 1914-1915. New York, Doubleday, 1935, 409p.

GARNER, JAMES W. International Law and the World War. New York, Longmans, 1920, 2v.

GREY, EDWARD GREY, 1st VISCOUNT. Twenty-five Years, 1892-1916. New York, Stokes, 1925, 2v.

HENDRICK, BURTON J. The Life and Letters of Walter H. Page. New York, Doubleday, 1922-1926, 3v. in 4 parts.

HOUSE, EDWARD M. Intimate Papers. Boston, Houghton, 1926-1928, 4v.

LANSING, ROBERT. War Memoirs. Indianapolis, Bobbs, 1935, 383p.

MILLIS, WALTER. Road to War: America, 1914-1917. Boston, Houghton, 1935, 466p.

Papers Relating to the Foreign Relations of the United States: The World War. Supplements to 1914, 1915, 1916 and 1917. Washington, Government Printing Office, 1928-1932.

SEYMOUR, CHARLES. American Diplomacy during the World War. Baltimore, Johns Hopkins Press, 1934, 417p.

—————. American Neutrality, 1914-1917. New Haven, Yale University Press, 1935, 187p.

U. S. DEPARTMENT OF STATE.. Neutrality Proclamations, 1914-1918. Washington, Government Printing Office, 1919, 64p.

Periodicals:

BAILEY, THOMAS A. The Sinking of the Lusitania. (In *American Historical Review,* October, 1935, p. 54-73.)

PHILLIPS, ETHEL C. American Participation in Belligerent Commercial Controls 1914-1917. (In *American Journal of International Law,* October, 1933, p. 675-693.)

SEYMOUR, CHARLES. American Neutrality: Experience of 1914-1917. (In *Foreign Affairs,* October, 1935, p. 26-36.)

POST WAR PERIOD

Books:

AMERICAN SOCIETY OF INTERNATIONAL LAW. Proceedings of the 27th Annual Meeting, April 27-29, 1933. Washington, The Society, 1933. (Includes addresses on neutrality by Charles Warren and Philip C. Jessup.)

——————. Proceedings of the 29th Annual Meeting, April 25-27, 1935. Washington, The Society, 1935. (Including addresses by: E. D. Dickinson, J. Dickinson, J. L. King, F. K. Nielson, James Brown Scott, Henry L. Stimson and L. H. Woolsey.)

INTERNATIONAL AMERICAN CONFERENCE, 6TH HAVANA, 1928. Maritime Neutrality. Convention between the United States of America and Other American Republics. Signed at Habana, February 20, 1928. Washington, Govt. Printing Office, 1932, 9p. (Treaty Series, No. 845.)

JESSUP, PHILIP C. American Neutrality and International Police. Boston, 1928, 170p. (World Peace Foundation Pamphlets, V. 11, No. 3.)

ROYAL INSTITUTE OF INTERNATIONAL AFFAIRS. Sanctions; the Character of International Sanctions and Their Application. London, The Institute, 1935, 64p.

SHEPARDSON, WHITNEY H. and SCROGGS, W. O. United States in World Affairs, 1934-1935. New York, Council on Foreign Relations, 1935, 357p.

UNITED STATES PRESIDENT, 1929-1933 (HOOVER). Address of President Hoover at the Ceremonies on the Eleventh Anniversary of Armistice Day . . . November 11, 1929. Washington, Government Printing Office, 1929, 7p.

UNITED STATES PRESIDENT, 1933- (FRANKLIN D. ROOSEVELT). Elimination of Weapons of Offensive Warfare. Message from the President of the United States . . . to the Sovereigns and Presidents of Those Nations Participating in the Disarmament Conferences and the

World Monetary and Economic Conference. Washington, Government Printing Office, 1933, 6p. (73d Congress, 1st Session. House Document 36.)

WERTENBAKER, THOMAS J. The United States and the Next European War. Princeton, Herbert L. Baker Foundation, 1935, p. 5-16. (Faculty-Alumni Forum.)

WRIGHT, QUINCY. The United States and Neutrality. Chicago, Chicago University Press, 1935, 29p. (Public Policy Pamphlet No. 17.)

Periodicals:

BARUCH, BERNARD. Cash and Carry. (In *Today*, November 2, 1935, p. 6-7.)

BOYE, THORVALD. Shall a State Which Goes to War in Violation of the Kellogg-Briand Pact Have a Belligerent's Rights in Respect of Neutrals? (In *American Journal of International Law*, October, 1930, p. 766-770.)

BRADLEY, PHILLIPS. Current Neutrality Problems—Some Precedents, an Appraisal, and a Draft Statute. (In *American Political Science Review*, December, 1935, p. 1022-1041.)

CHAMBERLAIN, JOSEPH P. The Embargo Resolutions and Neutrality. New York, Carnegie Endowment for International Peace, 90p. (In *International Conciliation*, June, 1929, No. 251.)

CLARK, BENNETT CHAMP. Detour Around War. (In *Harpers*, December, 1935, p. 1-9.)

COUDERT, FREDERIC R. Is Neutrality a Safe Policy for America? (In *Proceedings of the Academy of Political Science*, 1934, p. 163-174.)

DAVIS, NORMAN H. World Stability and the Sanctity of Treaties. Address before *New York Herald Tribune* Forum on Current Problems, October 15, 1935. (In *New York Herald Tribune*, October 16, 1935, p. 15.)

DULLES, ALLEN. Cost of Peace. (In *Foreign Affairs*, July, 1934, p. 567-578.)

EAGLETON, CLYDE. Neutrality and the Capper Resolution. (In *New York University Law Review*, May, 1929, p. 346-364.)

FENWICK, CHARLES G. Neutrality and International Organization. (In *American Journal of International Law*, April, 1934, p. 334-339.)

FOREIGN POLICY REPORTS. New York, Foreign Policy Association.

> V. 4, No. 1. Neutral Rights and Maritime Law. 1928, 18p.
> V. 4, No. 2. American Neutrality and League Wars. 1928, 16p.
> V. 11, No. 3. American Neutrality in a Future War. 1935, 12p.

GREY, EDWARD GREY, 1ST VISCOUNT. Freedom of the Seas. (In *Foreign Affairs*, April, 1930, p. 325-335.)

INTERNATIONAL COMMISSION OF JURISTS. Public International Law, Projects to be Submitted for the Consideration of the Sixth International Conference of American States. (In *American Journal of International Law*, January, 1928, Special No., p. 234-239.)

JESSUP, PHILIP C. The New Neutrality Legislation. (In *American Journal of International Law*, October, 1935, p. 665-670.)

MOORE, JOHN BASSETT. Appeal to Reason. (In *Foreign Affairs*, July, 1933, p. 547-588.)

NATIONAL PEACE CONFERENCE. Tentative Redraft of the Neutrality Act of August 31, 1935. Prepared by a Committee, James T. Shotwell, Chairman. (In *New York Times*, December 26, 1935, p. 10-11.)

STIMSON, HENRY L. The Dangers of Neutrality: Letter to the Editor. (In *New York Times,* October 11, 1935.)

————. The Pact of Paris: Three Years of Development. (In *Foreign Affairs,* October, 1932, Special Supplement.)

WARREN, CHARLES. Belligerent Aircraft, Neutral Trade and Unpreparedness. (In *American Journal of International Law,* April, 1935, p. 197-205.)

————. Contraband and Neutral Trade. In *Proceedings of The Academy of Political Science,* 1934, p. 185-194.)

————. Prepare for Neutrality. (In *Yale Review,* March, 1935, p. 467-478.)

————. Safeguards to Neutrality. (In *Foreign Affairs,* January, 1936, p. 199-215.)

————. Troubles of a Neutral. (In *Foreign Affairs,* April, 1934, p. 377-394.)

INDEX

Adams, John, 25
Anglo-French loan of 1935, 88
Armaments, limitation of, American position on, 46
Arms embargoes. *See* Embargoes
Arms traffic, regulation of, 43; U. S. investigation of, 45; Geneva convention, 40; international statistics, 82n.
Ayres, Leonard, 88
Baker, Ray Stannard, 22, 86
Bankhead, John H., 41
Baruch, Bernard M., quoted, 112
Belgium, neutrality of, violated, 23, 33
Bernstorff, Count von, 25n, 30
Bethlehem Steel Corporation, 82
Bolivia, arms embargo against, 77
Borah, William E., 64, 65, 67
Boycott. *See* Sanctions
Briand-Kellogg Pact, effect of, on conception of neutrality, 3, 5; suggested revision, 46; consultation implied in, 47; invoked by Ethiopia, 47; discussion of obligations under, 52, 115-116
Bridgeport Projectile Company, 109

Bryan, William Jennings, views on contraband, 28; on neutrality, 30, 80, 81; on loans to belligerents, 86, 87
Callender, Harold, quoted, 73
Canada, 85
"Cash and Carry" policy, urged in trade with belligerents, 112-113
China, 77; arms shipments to, 50, 163
Churchill, Winston, 23
Clark, Bennett Champ, 67
Collective security, policy of U. S., 51-52
Connally, Thomas T., 85
Contraband, extension of term in World War, 27-30; in international law, 35
Coolidge, Calvin, 51
Cotton, unaffected by neutrality legislation of 1935, 40; distribution of world production of, 165
Croix de Feu, 75
Cuba, embargo on arms shipments to, 163
Davis, Norman H., 46
Declaration of London, 26, 27
Democratic party, platform of 1932 favors international consultation, 46
Discretion, Executive, in neutrality legislation, 38; arguments for and against, 82-84

INDEX

Dominican Republic, embargo on arms shipments to, 162

Embargoes, first American, 15-19, 162; arms embargoes against Latin American countries, 50, 51, 162-164; in legislation of 1935, 37-39; imposed by U. S. against Italy and Ethiopia, 58; by League States against Italy, 62-64; lifted by League States from Ethiopia, 62; imposed by U. S. against Bolivia and Paraguay, 77; difficulties in mandatory, 56, 57, 81-85, 93-104

Ethiopia. *See* Italo-Ethiopian dispute

Fletcher, Duncan U., 40n

France, treatment of neutrals in wars with Great Britain, 11-19

Freedom of the Seas, obsolescence of the idea, 36, 59

Genet, "Citizen" E. C., 12

Geneva Arms Traffic Convention, 40

Germany, treatment of neutrals during World War, 22, 23, 30-32

Gerry, Peter Goelet, 41

Great Britain, treatment of neutrals in wars with France, 11-19; in World War, 25-34; reverses policy in Italo-Ethiopian dispute, 74-76

Grey, Viscount, quoted, 27, 29

Harding, Warren G., 51

Hitchcock, Gilbert M., 25

Hoare, Sir Samuel, reverses British Ethiopian policy, 74-76

Honduras, embargo on arms shipments to, 163

Hoover, Herbert, 51

Hull, Cordell, on obligations under Briand-Kellogg Pact, 47-48; warns against travel on ships of belligerents, 60, 61; seeks to discourage trade with belligerents, 69-73, 108; statement on Italo-Ethiopian dispute, text, 152-155

"Implements of War," meaning of the term, 40

Italo-Ethiopian dispute, 56; Americans take sides, 33; stimulates interest in neutrality legislation, 44, 45; Ethiopia appeals to U. S., 47; actions of League concerning, 61, 62; American official attitude, 44-48, 58-76; text of Hull statement, 152-155; British attitude, 74-76

Italy, American trade with, 60-63, 69-73, 167. *See also* Italo-Ethiopian dispute

Index

Japan, 77, 85

Jay Treaty, 15

Jefferson, Thomas, views on American neutrality, 11, 12, 16-17; and the Embargo Act, 17

Jessup, Philip C., 104

Johnson Act of 1934, 42, 85, 86; text of, 132

Johnson, Hiram, 42, 85

Key war materials, 92, 93; statistics of world production of, 165

Lansing, Robert, 22, 31, 86

League of Nations, effect of Covenant on concept of neutrality, 2, 3; and problem of sanctions, 49; efforts to check Italian aggression in Ethiopia, 61, 62, 66

Lippmann, Walter, 74, 103

Loans and credits to belligerents, proposed ban on, 49, 55, 85-90, 114; Anglo-French loan of 1935, 88; U. S. securities legislation of 1935, 89. *See also* Johnson Act

Lusitania, sinking of, 80

Madison, James, 19

Manchuria, 5

McReynolds, Sam D., 49, 53

Mexico, 50, 85; embargoes on arms shipments to, 163-164

Millis, Walter, 22, 23, 26, 109

Moral suasion, deemed inadequate for controlling war trade, 107-110

Morgan, J. P. and Company, 86

Morris, Gouverneur, 11

Munitions, meaning of term, 51. *See also* Arms traffic

Munitions Control Board, 43

Mussolini, Benito. *See* Italo-Ethiopian dispute

Neutrality, popular ideas concerning, 7; changing views of, 8, 9; Jefferson's conception of, 11, 12; Washington's proclamation of, 12; American view of neutral duties, 13-14, 59-61, 65f.; Jefferson and Wilson on neutral rights, 59; question of, during World War, 58-61, 65-69, 71-74, 79-81; President Wilson on neutral duties, 123-131; Warren proposals for American policy, 52-56; President F. D. Roosevelt's statement, text, 150-151; Secretary Hull's statement of Italo-Ethiopian dispute, text, 155; effects on, of Briand-Kellogg Pact, 47, 51-52; relation to, of League Covenant, 51; future American policy, 77-90

INDEX

Neutrality laws, Acts of 1794 and 1818, 14, 78; Act of 1917, 78-79; codified law of 1935, 133-142; bills in Congress in 1935, 48, 49; in 1936, text of, 168-178; Joint Resolution of 1935, 56-57, 79-81; text, 143-149; President F. D. Roosevelt's interpretations of, 58-76, 150-151; text of proclamations making Resolution effective, 156-161; attitude of Senators, 64-68; European reaction, 73, 74; extension and amendment, 1936, text of, 179-180

Nicaragua, embargo on arms shipments to, 163

Non-Intercourse Act, 18, 19

Nye Committee. *See* Nye, Gerald P.

Nye, Gerald P., 43, 45, 65

Oil, unaffected by neutrality legislation of 1935, 41; increase of shipments to Italy, 69, 70; League postpones extension of sanctions to shipments, 72; sources of supply, 92; data of world production, 165

Orders in Council, 14-19

Pact of Paris. *See* Briand-Kellogg Pact

Page, Walter Hines, quoted, 33

Paraguay, arms embargo against, 77

Pittman, Key, on scope of neutrality legislation of 1935, 40, 42

Quota system, proposed in lieu of embargoes on wartime exports, 110; objections to, 111-112

Recruiting, by foreign governments in U. S., 12, 55, 79

Roosevelt, Franklin D., 32, 61, 62; on neutrality legislation of 1935, 42, 56, 57, 58-76; texts of proclamations and statement relating thereto, 150-151, 156-161; warns Americans that trade with belligerents is at their own risk, 59; favors further restrictions on trade with belligerents, 68, 69

Roosevelt, Theodore, 33

Rule of War of 1756, 14

Sanctions, American attitude toward, 49, 61, 64-67, 71; applied by League to Italy, 62, 68, 72; change in British and French attitude, 74, 75

Seymour, Charles, 22

Sims, William S., quoted, 104, 105

Stimson, Henry L., on neutrality, 3n, 52

Stone, William J., 28, 87

Thomas, Elbert D., 66

Trade, rights of neutrals in time of war, 8, 11-19, 25-31; recent changes in American trade, 20, 21, 166; trade at own risk policy, 59, 104-107, 114; American sales of war material to Italy, 62-64, 69-73, 167; plans for control of war-time trade, 91-113

Travel, in war zones or on belligerents' vessels, 31, 32, 79-81

United States, early policy of neutrality, 11-19; efforts to be neutral in 1914-1917, 20-34; neutrality legislation of 1935, 35-57; attitude toward Italo-Ethiopian dispute, 44-48, 58-76; attitude toward League sanctions, 61, 63-67, 71; application of arms embargoes, 50, 58, 77, 162-164; control of arms traffic, 43; trade policy of, in time of war, 11-19, 55, 59-61, 65-69, 71, 91-113; changes in trade of, 20-21; trade with Italy, 60, 62-63, 69-73; trade with Ethiopia, 73; foreign loan policy, 86-90

Vandenberg, Arthur H., 66, 67-68

War of 1812-14, 14-19

Warren, Charles, proposals for American neutrality policy, 52-56, 104

Washington, George, issues neutrality proclamation, 12-14

Washington Treaties, 51

Wheat, unaffected by neutrality legislation of 1935, 41; distribution of world production of, 165

Wilson, Woodrow, efforts to maintain neutral rights, 32, 59, 81; on war loans, 87; proclamation and statement on neutrality, texts, 123-131

World War, effects of, on neutrality, 2, 20-34, 78, 84, 86-88; President Wilson on neutrality at outbreak of, 123-131